An Eagle's Flight

An Eagle's Flight

Sandra (Lott) Smith

Your New Life Ministries LLC

"But those who hope in the Lord will renew their strength.
They will soar on wings like eagles;
they will run and not grow weary,
they will walk and not be faint." Isaiah 40:31

Contents

Prologue

The wind flows with ease and at other times it is a mighty force in which anything it touches is changed. The eagle flies through the air with such grace. He looks regal with his wings spread wide, as he soars through the air. The eagle portrays strength and dignity, confidence and assuredness, as he soars ever higher. His flight is noble with a sense of pride evident in his demeanor. To look at an eagle fly is to watch with awe and wonder. The eagle has an air of strength and power about him, and a look of royalty.

Power, strength, and royalty: these describe our Almighty Heavenly Father. Just like a powerful wind, whomever God touches is changed. When the Almighty touches you, you are changed eternally. When God touches your heart and changes you, if you let Him continually mold you, the life you lead will be like that of an eagle's flight.

You can fly through life on the wings of an eagle, on the wings of our God.

(Exodus 19:4) "You yourselves have seen what I did to Egypt, and how I carried you on eagles' wings and brought you to Myself."

As you fly through life on the wings of our God, trusting in Him, you will be confident that you are His child. You will feel His loving presence within you, and you will see and trust in His love as He gives you strength and the ability to overcome each trial. Each trial that you overcome helps you to grow and mature. Just like a fledgling, a young eagle just learning to fly; with each flight, he gets better and better and more sure of himself. The same air of dignity will shine through your spirit with the aroma of the love and compassion of Jesus Christ.

(II Corinthians 2:15) "For we are to God the aroma of Christ among those who are being saved and those who are perishing."

As you soar through life—just as the mighty eagle flies proud and sure of his ability to get to his next destination, you will have that same confidence within you. You will trust beyond a shadow of a doubt that God's love and strength will always hold you up.

(Psalm 145:14) "The Lord upholds all those who fall and lifts up all who are bowed down."

God's grace is sufficient for you.

(II Corinthians 12:9) "My grace is sufficient for you, for My power is made perfect in weakness."

You will carry yourself in all situations with the same sense of pride in yourself that the eagle has; not pride in yourself in an arrogant way, but with confidence and pride in being a child of God.

As you read through the pages of this book, examine yourself and take your weaknesses to God. He will strengthen you in those areas. He did not send Jesus to die on the cross for our sins, just so you could struggle and have an unfruitful life. No! He died so that you would have an abundant life.

(John 10:10) "I have come that they may have life, and have it to the full." His plan for you involves a life of victory!
(I Corinthians 15:57) "He gives us the victory through our Lord Jesus Christ."

Take flight in the Spirit of God through the blood of Jesus Christ, and as you take shelter in the wings of the Almighty, your life will mimic an Eagle's Flight.

On the Wings of an Eagle

When the problems I face are too much to bear,
I know that He cares.
In my weakness, He's my strength.
He lifts me upon the Wings of an Eagle
and on His love
my heart feels lighter than air.
On the Wings of an Eagle
we soar through the air,
through the clouds, we ride
and now my problems seem so small.
In my weakness, He's my strength
His love will not let me fall.
When I feel overwhelmed
He's the one I run to,
the only One I need.
In His strength, I can carry on.
He guides me through life
On the Wings of an Eagle
His love carries me.

1

Courtship God's Calling

The Second Continental Congress officially declared the bald eagle the National Emblem of the United States in 1782. The bald eagle has since become the living symbol of the United States' freedoms, spirit, and pursuit of peace. Freedom from the bondage of sin and the heaviness you feel in your heart as you carry sin's heavy weight day in and day out is what becoming a child of God through faith in Jesus Christ gives you. (Galatians 5:1) "It is for freedom that Christ has set us free. Stand firm, then, and do not let yourselves be burdened again by a yoke of slavery." In Jesus, we are the righteousness of God and are free! (John 8:36) "So if the Son sets you free, you will be free indeed." (Philippians 3:8-9) "I consider everything a loss compared to the surpassing greatness of knowing Christ Jesus my Lord, for whose sake I have lost all things. I consider them rubbish, that I may gain Christ and be found in Him, not having a righteousness of my own that comes from the law, but that which is through faith in Christ—the righteousness that comes from God and is by faith." We can say "no" to sin with ease. (Titus 2:11-14) "For the grace of God that brings salvation has appeared to all men. It teaches us to say 'no' to ungodliness and worldly passions and to live self-controlled, upright, and godly lives in this present age while we wait for the blessed hope—the glorious appearing of our great God and Savior, Jesus Christ.

He is the one who gave Himself for us to redeem us from all wickedness and to purify for Himself a people that are His very own, eager to do what is good." The bald eagle is a symbol of royalty, power, and freedom; all of which we receive as a child of God. These are all traits of our Heavenly Father. So, it is no wonder that our founding fathers founded our country on the basis of "In God we trust," and this is printed on our currency in that belief, and in obedience and thanks to God. In the Declaration of Independence, our founding fathers gave glory to God. Here is an excerpt of it:

IN CONGRESS, July 4, 1776

The Unanimous Declaration of the Thirteen United States of America,

When in the Course of human events, it becomes necessary for one people to dissolve the political bands which have connected them with another, and to assume among the powers of the earth, the separate and equal station to which the Laws of Nature and of Nature's God entitle them, a decent respect to the opinions of mankind requires that they should declare the causes which impel them to the separation.

We hold these truths to be self-evident, that all men are created equal, that they are endowed by their Creator with certain unalienable Rights that among these are Life, Liberty, and the pursuit of Happiness.

If you read the Ten Commandments and compare them to the laws of our country, "Thou shalt not steal," thou shalt not kill," you will see that is where the laws originated from. Thanksgiving was started by our founding fathers offering up a day of thanksgiving unto God in a proclamation of the United States.

This is Abraham's Thanksgiving Proclamation:

Writing to President Abraham Lincoln, magazine editor Sarah J. Hale urged him to set a "day of our annual Thanksgiving made a National and fixed Union Festival." She wrote, "You may have observed that, for some years past, there has been an increasing interest felt in our land to have the Thanksgiving held on the same day, in all the States; it now needs National recognition and authoritative fixation, only, to become permanently, an American custom and institution."

According to Lincoln's secretary John Nicolay, this document was written by Secretary of State William Seward, and the original was in his handwriting.

Text of the Thanksgiving Proclamation

Washington, D.C. October 3, 1863 By the President of the United States of America.

A Proclamation

The year that is drawing towards its close, has been filled with the blessings of fruitful fields and healthful skies. To these bounties, which are so constantly enjoyed that we are prone to forget the source from which they come, others have been added, which are of so extraordinary a nature that they cannot fail to penetrate and soften even the heart which is habitually insensible to the ever-watchful providence of Almighty God. In the midst of a civil war of unequaled magnitude and severity, which has sometimes seemed to foreign States to invite and to provoke their aggression, peace has been preserved with all nations, order has been maintained, the laws have been respected and obeyed, and harmony has prevailed everywhere except in the theatre of military conflict; while that theatre has been greatly contracted by the advancing armies and navies of the Union. Needful diversions of wealth and of strength from the fields of peaceful industry to the national defense have not arrested the plough, the shuttle, or the ship; the axe has enlarged the borders of our settlements, and the mines, as well of iron and coal as of the precious metals, have yielded even more abundantly than heretofore. Population has steadily increased, notwithstanding the waste that has been made in the camp, the siege, and the battle-field; and the country, rejoicing in the consciousness of augmented strength and vigor, is permitted to expect continuance of years with large increase of freedom. **No human counsel hath devised nor hath any mortal hand worked out these great things. They are the gracious gifts of the Most High God**, *who, while dealing with us in anger for our sins, hath nevertheless, remembered mercy. It has seemed to me fit and proper that they should be solemnly, reverently, and gratefully acknowledged as with one heart and one voice by the whole American People. I do therefore invite my fellow citizens in every part of the United States, and also those who are at sea and those who are sojourning in foreign lands, to set apart and observe the* **last Thursday of November next, as a day of Thanksgiving and Praise to our beneficent Father who dwelleth in the Heavens.** *And I recommend to them that while offering up the ascriptions justly due to Him for such singular deliverances and blessings, they do also, with humble penitence for* *our national perverseness and disobedience, commend to His tender care all those who have become widows, orphans, mourners or sufferers in the lamentable civil strife in which we are unavoidably engaged, and fervently implore the interposition of the Almighty Hand to heal the wounds of the nation and to restore it as soon as may be consistent with the Divine purposes to the full enjoyment of peace, harmony, [tranquility] and Union.*

In testimony whereof, I have hereunto set my hand and caused the Seal of the United States to be affixed.

Done at the City of Washington, this Third day of October, in the year of our Lord one thousand eight hundred and sixty- three, and of the Independence of the United States the Eighty-eighth.

By the President: Abraham Lincoln

William H. Seward, Secretary of State

The bald eagle carries a lot of symbolism between our country's beliefs, the beliefs of Native American Indians, and the traits found in our Heavenly Father. The Native American Indians hold the eagle in the highest honor and have a true "heart and soul desire" to keep it flying healthy and free. Most Native American Indians attach special importance to the eagle and its feathers. Pictures of eagles and their feathers are used on many tribal logos as symbols of the Native American Indian. To be given an eagle feather is the highest honor that can be awarded within native cultures. Just as when you receive Jesus Christ as Lord of your life, you receive the highest honor. You become a child of God! (John 1:12) "Yet to all who received Him, to those who believe in His name, He gave the right to become children of God." Eagle feathers are never to be abused, disrespected, dropped, or contaminated. Just as a child of God, we are to turn our backs and leave our old lives of sin. (Ephesians 4:22-24) "You were taught, with regard to your former way of life, to put off your old self, which is being corrupted by its deceitful desires; to be made new in the attitude of your minds; and to put on the new self, created to be like God in true righteousness and holiness." God knows lip service. (Isaiah 29:13) "These people come near to Me with their mouth and honor Me with their lips, but their hearts are far from Me." Only real true men and women carry the eagle feather.

When we come to Jesus to accept Him as Lord we receive His gift of salvation and His protection and watchful eye over us forever, eternally. (Psalm 121:7) "The Lord will keep you from all harm—He will watch over your life; the Lord will watch over your coming and going both now and forevermore." When the Holy Spirit starts convicting you through a person or maybe questions in your spirit due to circumstances in your life causing you to hit rock bottom, you will have an encounter with God, and the Holy Spirit will keep leading or courting you until you submit and make Him Lord of your life. (Deuteronomy 32:10-12) "In a desert land, He found him, in a barren and howling waste. He shielded him and cared for him; He guarded him as the apple of His eye, like an eagle that stirs up its nest and hovers over its young, that spreads its wings to catch them and carries them on its pinions. The Lord alone led him; no foreign god was with him." When you are in that desert wasteland where your heart feels empty and dead, look up to Jesus and receive His gift: life everlasting. Pinions are the part of the bird's wings that allow them to change directions. That is what you are given the chance to do when you receive God's grace and His gift of salvation through Jesus Christ our Lord. You are given the chance to change directions from a path leading to destruction to one blessed by God and life everlasting. Who would not want that? Salvation is a gift; it is free, all you have to do is ask and be sincere to receive it. God wants true sincere worship.

(John 4:24) "God is spirit, and His worshipers must worship Him in spirit and in truth." We must draw near to Him with a sincere heart believing that He is who He says He is, and He did what He said that He did, even if we were the only ones left on earth. (Hebrews 10:22) "Let us draw near to God with a sincere heart in full assurance of faith, having our hearts sprinkled to cleanse us from a guilty conscience and having our bodies washed with pure water."

For the child of God who has been saved for a while, do you remember the time leading up to when you were saved? Do you remember the questions you may have started to ask yourself or the people you came in contact with who were Christians? Do you remember the impact they had on your life by how they lived? Maybe they witnessed to you. Do you remember certain things people said, or maybe you started becoming more and more aware of the emptiness inside and started wondering why and how to get rid of it?

Jesus came into the world to reconcile us to God. (Colossians 1:22) "But now He has reconciled you by Christ's physical body through death to present you holy in His sight, without blemish and free from accusation." He came that we might have life and have it to the full, to set us free from the bondage of sin and have life everlasting. (John 10:10) "I have come that they may have life, and have it to the full." God knew that with our sinful nature, we would never be able to pay for our sins, so He did it for us. (Isaiah 59:16) "He saw that there was no one, He was appalled that there was no one to intervene; so His own arm worked salvation for Him, and his own righteousness sustained Him."

The leadings and questions in your spirit are the callings and promptings of the Holy Spirit. (John 16:8) "When He comes, He will convict the world of guilt in regard to sin and righteousness and judgment." Bald eagles have a time of courtship before mating; this courtship is their way of winning the affection of another eagle. The eagle courtship is a sight to behold. They do a sky dance; the two birds soar and wheel, dip, and climb, come together, and glide apart. These sky dances are a prelude to actual mating, which does not take place until the nest has been completed. In their courtship display, they lock talons and cartwheel through the air for several hundred feet. The Lord does this through the working of the Holy Spirit and through His written and spoken Word. (John 16:13) "But when He, the Spirit of truth, comes, He will guide you into all truth." Before being saved we are all blind. (Isaiah 6:9-10) "Be ever hearing, but never understanding; be ever seeing, but never perceiving.

Make the heart of this people calloused; make their ears dull and close their eyes. Otherwise, they might see with their eyes, hear with their ears, understand with their hearts, and turn and be healed." The god of this world, Satan, blinds all those who are not saved, do not believe, or have too many gods such as drugs, alcohol, sex, or even TV or food. Whatever you run to for your peace, whatever you give excessive devotion to is a parallel to idol worship. If you fit into one of these categories or maybe something else other than the Almighty Father in heaven, then ask if Jesus is the Lord of your life. (II Corinthians 4:4) "The god of this age has blinded the minds of unbelievers, so they cannot see the light of the gospel, of the glory of Christ, who is the image of God."

The things that you start to question and feel in your spirit that may be wrong are examples of the ways that God, though you are blind, is leading you to call upon Jesus and be saved. (Isaiah 42:16) "I will lead the blind by ways they have not known, along unfamiliar paths I will guide them; I will turn the darkness into light before them and make the rough places smooth. These are the things I will do; I will not forsake them." God does not want anyone to perish. He wants all men to be saved. (II Peter 3:9) "He is patient with you, not wanting anyone to perish, but everyone to **come** to repentance." Just as the Lord called on Lazarus to come forth, He will lead you (through the questions and the emptiness)toward His path until you call on the name of Jesus and receive His free gift of salvation. (Joel 2:32) "And everyone who calls on the name of the Lord will be saved." One could identify the funeral bindings Lazarus had on as a part of the burial ritual with the things that bind us—the misconstrued views we have about day-to-day events or common misconceptions about things that people do to us or things that have happened to us in the past. The Lord called upon others to unbind Lazarus of his funeral wrappings, so remember that He does not expect us to do this thing called Christianity totally on our own. We do have His Spirit with us and fellow brothers and sisters in the faith.

The Lord will cause certain events to happen, as He did with Jonah when he thought that he could run from God and still have peace! He ran from the Creator of the universe, the One who alone has the power to give life or take it away, and he thought that he could run from God and get away with it! Kind of funny, isn't it? He found out in the Book of Jonah 2:2 that when God sent him to his own personal hell, being swallowed by a fish, Jonah gave up and cried out to God, "In my distress, I called to the Lord, and He answered me. From the depths of the grave I called for help, and You listened to my cry." God does not want us to suffer. Why do you think He sent Jesus to pay the price for our sins? If He wanted us to suffer, He would have stayed home. We make things harder than they have to be. But if we persist and do not heed His calling, He will find a way to get our attention, even if it hurts. (II Thessalonians 2:13) "God chose you to be saved through the sanctifying work of the Spirit and through belief in the truth." As parents we can testify to that; we do not want to punish our children, but if they do not obey, we punish them. God does this also so we will not have to suffer an eternity in hell. (Job 33:29-30) "God does all these things to a man—twice, even three times—to turn his soul from the pit that the light of life may shine on him." Different things will happen, or you will hear a word from somewhere, or you will start asking yourself different questions. These are all ways God will speak to your heart. (Job 33:14-18) "For God does speak—now one way, now another—though man may not perceive it. In a dream, in a vision of the night, when deep sleep falls on men as they slumber in their beds, He may speak in their ears and terrify them with warnings, to turn man from wrongdoing and keep him from pride, to preserve his soul from the pit, his life from perishing by the sword."

There are no coincidences in life. A man's steps are directed by God, and the consequences that you reap are from what you have sown. (Proverbs 20:24) "A man's steps are directed by the Lord. How then can anyone understand his own way?" The Lord loves us so much that He died for us. He alone paid the price that we ourselves should pay. (Romans 5:8) "But God demonstrates His own love for us in this: While we were still sinners, Christ died for us." He will do anything to get our attention to save our souls, just as you would do the same for your children or someone you love. (Isaiah 30:30) "The Lord will cause men to hear His majestic voice and will make them see His arm coming down." God will direct your heart, your mind, and different events in your life to get your attention so that you may know His love. (II Thessalonians 3:5) "May the Lord direct your hearts into God's love and Christ's perseverance." If He would take the punishment heaped on Him, the insults, the beatings, and His hands and feet **NAILED TO A CROSS** (what agony), then that alone should speak of His awesome love for us! (Ephesians 3:17-19) "I pray that you, being rooted and established in love, may have power, together with all the saints, to grasp how wide and long and high and deep is the love of Christ, and to know this love that surpasses knowledge— that you may be filled to the measure of all the fullness of God."

Our Heavenly Father will do anything to get your attention. These events—good or bad—as the eagle that courts its soon-to-be-mate, are God's way of courting you. His Holy Spirit will testify to your heart as He calls you. (John 15:26) "The Spirit of truth who goes out from the Father, He will testify about Me." He called out to Lazarus to "come forth," and he rose from the dead. He is calling out to you to do the same. (Ephesians 5:14) "Wake up, O sleeper, **rise** from the dead, and Christ will shine on you." He will not wait forever, and He alone knows the hour and time of your death and the day He comes to take His people home before the Tribulation. (Job 14:5) "Man's days are determined; you have decreed the number of his months and have set limits he cannot exceed."

Putting God off for momentary pleasures of the world could, by your own rejection of Christ, send you to hell. (Jonah 2:8) "Those who cling to worthless idols forfeit the grace that could be theirs." The hour of Tribulation draws closer and closer as satellite allows us to reach the world with the gospel of Christ. (Matthew 24:14) "And this gospel of the kingdom will be preached in the whole world as a testimony to all nations, and then the end will come." Matthew chapter 24 also tells of growing pains that will happen as the end draws near. This is happening, listen to your news. (Isaiah 55:6-7) "Seek the Lord while He may be found; call on Him while He is near. Let the wicked forsake his way and the evil man his thoughts. Let him turn to the Lord, and He will have mercy on him and to our God, for He will freely pardon." Are you ready?

(Isaiah 26:19-21) "But your dead will live; their bodies will rise. You who dwell in the dust, wake up and shout for joy. Your dew is like the dew of the morning; the earth will give birth to her dead. Go, My people, enter your rooms and shut the doors behind you; hide yourselves for a little while until His wrath has passed by. See, the Lord is coming out of His dwelling to punish the people of the earth for their sins." This "little while" and this "wrath" is the

Seven Year Tribulation. Do you want to be taken away to be with the Lord and your saved loved ones and avoid the Great Tribulation? If you think things are getting bad now, wait around; during the seven years of Tribulation, it will be a lot worse. What personal hell is God going to have to put you through to save you from eternal damnation? It doesn't have to be that way. (Psalm 95:8) "Today, if you hear His voice, do not harden your hearts as you did at Meribah." You choose the path by your own stubbornness or submission. (Jeremiah 6:16) "Stand at the cross-roads and look; ask for the ancient paths, ask where the good way is, and walk in it, and you will find rest for your souls." Do you want to wander in the desert of restlessness or do you want to know personally the love and the peace of God that could be yours? (Psalm 95:10-11) "For forty years I was angry with that generation; I said, 'They are a people whose hearts go astray, and they have not known My way.' So I declared on oath in My anger, 'They shall never enter My rest.'"

The days are getting shorter and the time for God's wrath approaches as men grow colder and colder, further and further away from God's everlasting love. (II Thessalonians 3:4) "Don't let anyone deceive you in any way, for that day will not come until the rebellion occurs and the man of lawlessness is revealed, the man doomed to destruction. He will oppose and will exalt himself over everything that is called God or is worshiped, so that he sets himself up in God's temple, proclaiming him-self to be God." (II Timothy 3:1-5) "But mark this: There will be terrible times in the last days. People will be lovers of themselves, lovers of money, boastful, proud, abusive, disobedient to their parents, ungrateful, unholy, without love, unforgiving, slanderous, without self-control, brutal, not lovers of the good, treacherous, rash, conceited, lovers of pleasure rather than lovers of God—having a form of godliness but denying its power. Have nothing to do with them." Do you want to be carried away with the rest of God's church, or do you want to be left behind to suffer God's wrath? The choice is yours. (Joel 3:13-14) "Swing the sickle, for the harvest is ripe. Come, trample the grapes, for the winepress is full, and the vats overflow—so great is their wickedness! Multitudes, multitudes in the valley of decision! For the day of the Lord is near in the valley of decision."

God will not court you forever. There will come a day as He did with the Israelites coming into the promised land. Twelve spies were sent in to scope out the land. You would think that after parting the Red Sea, they would trust in God's awesome power to deliver them—not so. They still doubted. Ten came back fearful, only Joshua and Caleb came back saying that with God they would gain the victory. They paid the price for their doubt. Their children and Joshua and Caleb and their families were allowed to enter, but the ones who doubted were not. Do you want to be turned away from heaven for an eternity? That is a long time...forever. (Deuteronomy 1:45) "You came back and wept before the Lord, but He paid no attention to your weeping and turned a deaf ear to you."

He wants to carry you on His shoulders through life in the love and light of His grace. As things happen in your life, instead of getting upset at them, ask yourself, ask God "What does this mean?" Ask, "What am I doing wrong, or what am I not doing and what direction are You trying to lead me in?" God your Father wants to carry you through life on the wings of His love. Let Him. He is just a prayer away. (Exodus 19:4) "You yourselves have seen what I did to Egypt, and how I carried you on eagles wings and brought you to Myself." In your weakness, His strength will shine through. (II Corinthians 12:9) "My grace is sufficient for you, for My power is made perfect in weakness."

2

∽

The Scales Removed Your Eyes Opened!

If you were not saved before reading the first chapter and since have asked Jesus into your heart, you have made the right choice! Rejoice, for now, your eternal home is in heaven! Go ahead and praise God! He deserves it! You are now saved! You will now notice, or if you are already saved, I am sure that you have already experienced a newfound understanding of God's Word. God has revealed Himself to you and your heart. (John 17:6) "I have revealed You to those whom You gave Me out of the world." Spiritual things seem to make more sense to you. This is due to the veil being removed, and now your eyes are opened; you have now received your spiritual eyesight. (II Corinthians 3:15-16) "Even to this day when Moses is read, a veil covers their hearts. But whenever anyone turns to the Lord, the veil is taken away."

When you lived according to the pleasures of the world and habitual sin, Satan blinded your eyes to the truths of God. (II Corinthians 4:4) "The god of this age has blinded the minds of unbelievers so that they cannot see the light of the gospel of the glory of Christ, who is the image of God." In accepting Jesus, He opens your eyes and now you see and understand! The scales have been removed from your eyes! The Book of

17

Acts tells how Saul became Paul as he was on his way to persecute more Christians in Damascus. The Lord stopped him on the way. Seeing the Lord in his glory, Saul was blinded for three days. Just as three days after His death, Jesus Christ rose from the dead to His eternal glory and for our salvation! After three days Saul received his sight when a disciple named Ananias placed his hands on him. Saul became a new creation in Christ, and his name was changed to Paul. Before receiving Christ we are sinners; afterward, we are the righteousness of Christ! The scales have been removed from Paul's eyes, and now he sees, understands, and knows who Jesus Christ is! (Acts 9:17-19) "Then Ananias went to the house and entered it. Placing his hands on Saul, he said, 'Brother Saul, the Lord—Jesus, who appeared to you on the road as you were coming here—has sent me so that you may see again and be filled with the Holy Spirit.' Immediately, something like scales fell from Saul's eyes, and he could see again. He got up and was baptized, and after taking some food, he regained his strength." Give glory to God!

In reading the Bible, the things that you found hard to understand before now seem to make sense to you. This is due to the Holy Spirit within you, giving you new light, wisdom, and understanding. (Daniel 2:21-22) "He gives wisdom to the wise and knowledge to the discerning. He reveals deep and hidden things; He knows what lies in darkness and light dwells with Him." (Proverbs 1:7) "The fear of the Lord is the beginning of knowledge, but fools despise wisdom and discipline." Where things once seemed dark, now there is light, and the joy and the peace of the Lord are in your heart. (Psalm 97:11) "Light is shed upon the righteous and joy in the upright in heart."

Young eagles that are just born are called eaglets. Their feathers are more of a thick layer of down. It is a fluffy coating that will keep them warm until their normal feathers grow in. The eyes of young eaglets are brown and their beaks are black until they reach the age of four or five. Then their eyes and beaks turn yellow. Eaglets are helpless during the first few weeks after they are born. They cannot stand or walk in the nest. Just like us when we are "born again," we now have new sight, but we are baby Christians. (John 3:5-7) "I tell you the truth; no one can enter the kingdom of God unless he is born of water and the Spirit. Flesh gives birth to flesh, but the Spirit gives birth to spirit. You should not be surprised at My saying, 'You must be born again."

We need continual study in the Word. (John 6:35) "I am the bread of life. He who comes to Me will never go hungry, and he who believes in Me will never be thirsty." He will not only meet our physical needs, but our spiritual needs as well. The Word is our strength and will help us to keep growing in Christ and have fighting power against Satan, just as eaglets need their flying feathers before they can fly.

Some birds are born unclothed, but not the bald eagle. The bald eagle is born fully clothed with a coat of pale gray down. The head and the underparts of the eaglet are pure white. When we become a child of God, our hearts, once stained with sin, become as pure white, purified by the blood of Jesus Christ. (I John 1:7) "But if we walk in the light, as He is in the light, we have fellowship with one another, and the blood of Jesus, His Son, purifies us from all sin." Not only are we purified; we are fully clothed just as the baby eaglet. We are clothed with the Spirit of Jesus, which is deposited into our hearts at the moment of conversion, the moment you ask forgiveness of your sins and ask Jesus into your heart. (Galatians 4:6-7) "Because you are sons, God sent the Spirit of His Son into our hearts, the Spirit who calls out, '*Abba*, Father.' So you are no longer a slave, but a son; and since you are a son, God has made you also an heir." As we stay in the Word, pray, and talk to God daily, we will grow and change, and light will be shed on new areas of our lives as we grow and mature in Christ. (Psalm 139:11-12) "If I say, 'Surely the darkness will hide me and the light become night around me,' even the darkness will not be dark to you; the night will shine like the day, for darkness is as light to you."

The "courting" of God has made you aware of your sinful state and you have submitted your heart to Jesus as Lord and Savior of your life and soul. (Romans 3:23) "For we all have sinned and fall short of the glory of God and are justified freely by His grace through the redemption that came by Jesus Christ." When you see yourself through God's eyes, as different things happen to help you to see the truth, you realize that you, as with everyone else, in the light of God's glory and holiness, are a sinner. This will bring a godly sorrow into your heart and aid your decision to give your heart to God and ask for forgiveness of your sins. (II Corinthians 7:10) "Godly sorrow brings repentance that leads to salvation and leaves no regret, but worldly sorrow brings death." This truth sets your captive heart free! (John 8:32) "Then you will know the truth, and the truth will set you free." The hold that your habitual sins have on you is gone! (Psalm 146:7-8) "The Lord sets the prisoners free; the Lord gives sight to the blind." Your newfound love for God will make you want to obey Him. The revelation of just how much He suffered for us—for you and me—will flood your heart and soul like a river, and loving and obeying Him will be a privilege to you. (John 3:16) "For God so loved the world that He gave His one and only Son, that whoever believes in Him shall not perish but have eternal life."

Through revelation of Himself and His love for you, your eyes will be opened to things that were once hidden from you. (Isaiah 43:11-12) "I, even I, am the Lord, and apart from Me there is no savior. I have revealed and saved and proclaimed." (Isaiah 65:1) "I revealed Myself to those who did not ask for Me; I was found by those who did not seek Me." The lies and things that Satan had deceived you into believing have now become clear to you. (Job 28:11) "He searches the sources of the rivers and brings hidden things to light."

Baby eaglets are helpless when they are first born, and as new Christians, we are as well. We are totally dependent on God to unveil His truths to us. He does that through His Word. Baby eagles—and even us as children—have complete faith in their parents. We are to have that same faith in God. (Hebrews 11:6) "And without faith it is impossible to please God because anyone who comes to Him must believe that He exists and that He rewards those who earnestly seek Him." Satan will try to destroy that. (John 10:10) "The thief comes only to steal, kill and destroy; I have come that they may have life, and have it to the full." Staying in the Word will help to keep that from happening. (II Timothy 3:16-17) "All Scripture is God-breathed and is useful for teaching, rebuking, correcting and training in righteousness, so that the man of God may be thoroughly equipped for every good work." God created man, the world and every-thing in it, and the heavens above. (Genesis 1:1-2) " In the beginning, God created the heavens and the earth. Now the earth was formless and empty, darkness was over the surface of the deep, and the Spirit of God was hovering over the waters." God is Spirit, and so is His Word. All he had to do was say it and it was so. (Psalm 138:2) "For You have exalted above all things Your Name and Your Word." When we read the Bible and stand on God's promises, believing in faith, we will not only grow in Christ but the things that we pray for in line with His Word will be answered as well. (Mark 11:24) "Therefore I tell you, whatever you ask for in prayer, believe that you have received it, and it will be yours."

Speak His Word; stand on it in faith. Stand firm and beware; Satan will not sit idly by. He will try to steal from your heart and make you doubt through circumstances bombarding you. Don't fall for it! What are you going to believe—God's Word from the One who died for you, or the doubts that Satan will try to bombard your mind with? That is why you must stay in the Word. God spoke and it came to be. You can too, but you must give God time to bring it to pass. You cannot snap your fingers and expect God to jump to it. He is God and you are not. Always remember that, and speak out about what you believe in, even if you are not sure at first. Keep speaking it until you do. Faith comes by hearing. (Romans 10:17) " Faith comes from hearing the message, and the message is heard through the word of Christ." As you keep speaking it, soon your heart and mind will believe what you are praying for as well. (Genesis 1:3)"And God said, 'Let there be light,' and there was light." God had His Word first. (John 1:1-2) "In the beginning was the Word, and the Word was with God, and the Word was God. He was with God in the beginning." The Word of God is Jesus Christ. (John 1:14) "The Word became flesh and made His dwelling among us. We have seen His glory, the glory of the One and Only, who came from the Father, full of grace and truth." God's Word, the Bible, and Jesus Christ will sustain us through life if we trust in Him. (Luke 6:47-48) "I will show you what he is like who comes to Me and hears My Words and puts them into practice. He is like a man building a house, who dug down deep and laid the foundation on rock.

When a flood came, the torrent struck that house but could not shake it, because it was well built." Jesus Christ is the Rock, the foundation on which our faith is built. (Isaiah 28:16) "See, I lay a stone in Zion, a tested stone, a precious cornerstone for a sure foundation; the one who trusts will never be dismayed."

The baby eaglet has a new life and will grow and change. It will get new feathers in and soon will start moving around. As a new Christian, you will go through many changes, all for the glory of God. (Isaiah 43:7) "Everyone who is called by My name, whom I created for My glory, whom I formed and made." He breathed new life into you and will keep shedding light into your life as you stand firm in your faith and keep following Him. (Genesis 2:7) "The Lord formed the man from the dust of the ground and breathed into his nostrils the breath of life, and the man became a living being." If you let God change and mold you, you will be changed more and more into His image. You will be changed from glory to glory, and with each noticed change you will praise God for the new life that He gave you. (Romans 8:17-18) "Now if we are children, then we are heirs—heirs of God and co-heirs with Christ if indeed we share in His sufferings so that we may also share in His glory. I consider that our present sufferings are not worth comparing with the glory that will be revealed in us."

3

Overwhelming Love Birthed!

A baby eaglet has just been born. There is a new life within him. So it is with us when we are "born again" into the family of God. We have new desires birthed in us, an overwhelming love that comes from God, and God overflowing in our hearts. (I John 4:7-8) "Dear friends, let us love one another, for love comes from God. Everyone who loves has been born of God and knows God. Whoever does not love does not know God, because God is love."

Each day as a new Christian, Jesus becomes more and more real to you. You have new desires and joy and peace in your heart given to you by the Holy Spirit of Jesus Christ. (Galatians 5:22-23) "But the fruit of the Spirit is love, joy, peace, patience, kindness, goodness, faithfulness, gentleness and self-control." The peace and joy He gives are eternal; the peace you get from the world is temporary, lasting only for a moment, and then life hits you again. (II Corinthians 4:18) "So we fix our eyes not on what is seen, but on what is unseen. For what is seen is temporary, but what is unseen is eternal."

After the buzz from the drinking binge you went on wears off, or the food binge you went on is completed, or the shopping trip where you spent money that you did not have to spend, life slaps you in the face again and the problems are still there. You are a little more broke and still as empty inside with the same problems that you had before. In Jesus, He gives you peace and a promise in His Word that our every battle is won! (II Chronicles 20:15) "Do not be afraid or discouraged because of this vast army. For the battle is not yours, but God's." The Lord told the Israelites that they would not have to fight. This is a promise for us as well. (II Chronicles 20:17) "You will not have to fight this battle. Take up your positions; stand firm and see the deliverance the Lord will give you, O Judah and Jerusalem." The world's pleasures do not give you this promise. God will give you what you need to win every battle that you face. (Deuteronomy 8:18) "But remember the Lord your God, for it is He who gives you the ability to produce wealth, and so confirms His covenant, which He swore to your forefathers, as it is today." God will do what you cannot do. Trust Him for victory over every circumstance, whether it is financial, emotional, personal relationships, or spiritual. Whatever it is, God will give you what you need to overcome and will lead you through it to permanent victory.

The world does not give you this promise. (II Samuel 22:33) "It is God who arms me with strength and makes my way perfect." (I Corinthians 15:54-57) "Death has been swallowed up in victory. Where, O death, is your victory? Where, O death, is your sting? The sting of death is sin, and the power of sin is the law. But thanks be to God! He gives us the victory through our Lord Jesus Christ." Victory over sin and victory passing through our trials and in our answered prayers is an awesome promise of God and an overwhelming show of His love for us.

As you read through God's Word and stand on His promises you will see just how alive His Word is and how faithful God is to us as His children. You will see His overwhelming love more and more as each day passes and with each trial you overcome. Reading God's Word births new desires within you—not only to please Him and learn more but desires that will direct your learning process toward the path for your life that He has for you. (Ephesians 1:11-12) "In Him, we were chosen, having been predestined according to the plan of Him who works out everything in conformity with the purpose of His will, in order that we who were the first to hope in Christ, might be for the praise of His glory."

You have been born again and are now a new creation in Christ. (II Corinthians 5:17) "Therefore, if anyone is in Christ, He is a new creation." God has given you a new spirit and these new desires that come from God are not only for His purpose and plan and to help you grow, but they are to give you strength and keep you close to God. (Ezekiel 36:26) "I will give you a new heart and put a new spirit in you; I will remove from you your heart of stone and give you a heart of flesh." The closer you get to God, the less the world's pleasure will have a hold on you. When God sets you free, you are truly free. (John 8:36) "So if the Son sets you free, you will be free indeed."

Baby eaglets under the age of five look different from those that are five years or older. Taking care of the eaglets, feeding, etc., is shared by both parents until the eaglets are full-size at 12 weeks of age. As new Christians, we need God's abundant love and wisdom to teach and guide us as we start to grow. There is a season for everything, even trials. (Ecclesiastes 3:1) "There is a time for everything and a season for every activity under heaven." Even Jesus had a time of testing. (Matthew 4:1) "Then Jesus was led by the Spirit into the desert to be tempted by the devil."

Eagles do not have gizzards and are not able to digest vegetation, so they must kill everything they catch. They must be very strong and powerful to kill their prey. Satan, compared to us, is very powerful and we need the strength, power, and wisdom of God to overcome Satan's attacks with victory. We also need to put to death our old habitual way of life. (Colossians 3:5-10) "Put to death, therefore, whatever belongs to your earthly nature: sexual immorality, impurity, lust, evil desires, and greed, which is idolatry. Because of these, the wrath of God is coming. You used to walk in these ways, in the life you once lived. But now you must rid yourselves of all such things as these: anger, rage, malice, slander, and filthy language from your lips. Do not lie to each other, since you have taken off your old self with its practices and have put on the new self, which is being renewed in knowledge in the image of its Creator."

Surrender all to God and receive victory. his is for our good. Keeping any sinful ways will only prove to be your downfall. Sin, if not dealt with, will spread and grow like yeast and keep you burdened by a heavy weight of sin that in coming to Jesus, you rid yourself of. (Matthew 16:6) "'Be careful,' Jesus said to them. 'Be on your guard against the yeast of the Pharisees and Sadducees."   (I Corinthians 5:6) "Your boasting is not good. Don't you know that a little yeast works through the whole batch of dough?" Don't be enslaved again by keeping a few sinful habits! That is not the true victory Christ died to give us. We can only have complete victory over trials and sin with the Holy Spirit within us, which is only given through receiving Jesus as Lord. (John 15:5) "I am the vine; you are the branches. If a man remains in Me and I in him, he will bear much fruit; apart from Me you can do nothing."

Jesus went through testing, insults, and beatings, and He overcame them. Only through Him can we overcome as well. (John 16:33) "I have told you these things, so that in Me you may have peace. In this world, you will have trouble. But take heart! I have overcome the world." Before going through your time of testing, and during, trust God. He will prepare you and lead you through so you will have victory in every situation. (Psalm 44:3) "It was not by their sword that they won the land, nor did their arm bring them victory; it was Your right hand, Your arm, and the light of Your face, for You loved them."

Feeding eaglets is a full-time job for the parents. God knows the trouble we are about to face.   He has been through our trials ahead of us and already knows how and what to teach us and what impurities we have stored up in our hearts to clean out. (Deuteronomy 9:3) "But be assured today that the Lord your God is the one who goes across ahead of you like a devouring fire. He will destroy them; He will subdue them before you. And you will drive them out and annihilate them quickly, as the Lord has promised." You are already assured of the outcome. You win! You just have to go through and claim your answered prayer, your deliverance, your salvation, and your victory!

You have years of the world in you that the Lord needs to clean out. This is done through trials. (Matthew 15:13) "Every plant that my heavenly Father has not planted will be pulled up by the roots." In the early stages of being a Christian, God will show you in different ways the evidence of His presence to help build your faith. Eagle parents will care for their young until they have learned and mastered their flying skills. The Holy Spirit will guide you on your path of learning and cleansing or sanctifying. (John 16:13) "But when He, the Spirit of truth comes, He will guide you into all truth. He will not speak on His own; He will speak only what He hears, and He will tell you what is yet to come."

As you read the Word of God, the Holy Spirit will teach you and unlock the doors of your spiritual understanding so the Bible becomes alive to you. It will become your strength, your spiritual nourishment that you will not want to live without. (John 14:26) "But the Counselor, the Holy Spirit, whom the Father will send in My name, will teach you all things and will remind you of everything I have said to you." As the eagle parents keep a watchful eye on their young, God does the same for us. (Proverbs 15:3) "The eyes of the Lord are everywhere, keeping watch on the wicked and the good." God is always with us, and He has made us that promise in His Word. (Deuteronomy 31:6) "Be strong and courageous. Do not be afraid or terrified because of them, for the Lord your God goes with you; He will never leave you nor forsake you." The eagle parents supply what is needed for their young and protect them. There is no bird that is a more attentive parent than an eagle parent. As His child, God will always supply your needs, just as your parents did for you as a child growing up. When trials start, don't stop reading the Bible; it is your weapon against Satan. Satan knows the Word, and in Jesus' time of testing, he used it against Jesus.

That is kind of ignorant when you think about it; Satan used the Word of God against the Son of God, who was the Word who became flesh! (John 1:14) "The Word became flesh and made His dwelling among us. We have seen His glory, the glory of the One and Only who came from the Father, full of grace and truth."

You have the Spirit of Jesus within you, so when trouble comes, run to the only One who can bring you through with victory. (Psalm

46:1) "God is our refuge and strength and ever-present help in times of trouble."

Few species of birds feed their young over such a long period of time as the eagle. God continually watches over His children and will continue to do it until His work in us is finished, which is when we are called home to heaven! What an awesome God! (I Chronicles 28:20) "Be strong and courageous, and do the work. Do not be afraid or discouraged, for the Lord God, my God, is with you. He will not fail you or forsake you until all the work for the service of the temple of the Lord is finished." (Philippians 1:6) "Being confident of this, that He who began a good work in you will carry it on to completion until the day of Christ Jesus."

He says to stay in His Word, for it is our weapon against Satan. (Psalm 149:6) "May the praise of God be in their mouths and a double-edged sword in their hands." Stay in God's Word and fellowship, go to church regularly, and talk to God daily. This will keep you close to God and keep His strength and His power working strong in you to lead you through every trial with victory. (James 4:7-8) "Submit yourselves, then, to God. Resist the devil, and he will flee from you. Come near to God and He will come near to you." Make your daily prayer for God to teach you His ways. (Psalm 25:4-5) "Show me Your ways, O Lord, teach me Your paths; guide me in Your truth and teach me, for You are God my Savior, and my hope is in you all day long." His ways bring victory and everything needed to sustain you. (Matthew 6:33) "But seek first His kingdom and His righteousness, and all these things will be given to you as well."

A newly hatched eagle will not be able to walk until it is five weeks old, but it will waddle about until it can. God gives us His Word to use, but He will not make us. His Word is a light for our path, to be given to us to help us on life's path. (Psalm 119:105) "Your Word is a lamp to my feet and a light for my path."

We are going to go through trials and if we go through it with Jesus and God's way, we will go through victoriously. God gave us His Word as a blessing to us. We must put feet to our faith and use it for it to work for us. (James 2:17) "In the same way, faith by itself, if it is not accompanied by action, is dead."

In the world, you are going to have troubles, things that leave you hopeless, but as children of God, we have the hope and promise of victory and are clothed with His power and love. (Job 30:18) "In His great power God becomes like clothing to me; He binds me like the neck of my garment." (Isaiah 61:10) "For He has clothed me with garments of salvation and arrayed me in a robe of righteousness."

In Christ alone, we are made righteous and we are given rest as we place our trust in Him. (Isaiah 30:15) "In repentance and rest is your salvation, in quietness and trust is your strength." In Christ alone our outcome is guaranteed—we win! (Romans 8:31) "What, then, shall we say in response to this? If God is for us, who can be against us?" God is love, He has poured out all His love into our hearts and love never fails. (I John 4:16) "God is love." Love never lets you down. (I Corinthians 13:8) "Love never fails." God will prepare us for trials. He is not going to send His only Son to suffer the way He did and die for our sins, and then let us suffer in defeat through the rest of our life. Our trials will change us to be more like Him. (Romans 5:3-5) "Not only so, but we also rejoice in our sufferings, because we know that suffering produces perseverance; perseverance, character; and character, hope. And hope does not disappoint us, because God has poured out His love into our hearts by the Holy Spirit, whom He has given us."

God's "amazing grace" not only saves us, but it sustains us through life. How awesome is the love of God that He births into our hearts and lives so that we may live with Him in paradise, eternally! Praise God! (Titus 3:5-7) "He saves us through the washing of rebirth and renewal by the Holy Spirit, whom He poured out on us generously through Jesus Christ our Savior, so that, having been justified by His grace, we might become heirs having the hope of eternal life." God's "amazing grace," how sweet it is!

4

Fledgling; Starting To Grow & Trials Begin

The eagle is said to be able to fly higher and see better than any other bird, and therefore it is able to see things from a different perspective. Its wingspan is seven to eight feet, which helps the eagle to soar. In much the same way our heavenly Father sees things from a different perspective than we do and in Christ, we can soar ever higher through life. He is the Beginning and the End, the Alpha and Omega. He knows the beginning of our trial, and He knows the end. (Revelation 22:13-14) "I am the Alpha and the Omega, the First and the Last, the Beginning and the End. Blessed are those who wash their robes, that they may have the right to the tree of life and may go through the gates into the city." The "tree of life" is Jesus—our life and salvation, our mediator between God and us, and all who trust in Him will go through life victoriously. (Proverbs 3:5-6) "Trust in the Lord with all your heart and lean not on your own understanding; in all your ways acknowledge Him, and He will make your paths straight." (Hebrews 9:15) "For this reason Christ is the mediator of a new covenant, that those who are called may receive the promised eternal inheritance—now that He has died as a ransom to set them free from the sins committed under the first covenant."

Our God is God, He is the Almighty Creator, His ways are for an eternal glory and they are much higher than ours. (Isaiah 55:8-9) "'For My thoughts are not your thoughts, neither are your ways My ways,' declares the Lord. 'As the heavens are higher than the earth, so are My ways higher than your ways and My thoughts higher than your thoughts.'" In the Indian culture, the eagle is believed to be a messenger from God. The eagle is symbolized in the Bible in many passages to be a representation of our heavenly Father because of the sense of royalty that it has and the love that it has for its young. (Isaiah 40:31) "But those who hope in the Lord will renew their strength. They will soar on wings like eagles; they will run and not grow weary, they will walk and not be faint."

The Holy Spirit is our messenger from God; at conversion, the Holy Spirit is planted in our hearts, and our heavenly Father speaks to our hearts through the Holy Spirit within us. (John 16:13-15) "But when He, the Spirit of Truth, comes, He will guide you into all truth. He will not speak on His own; He will speak only what He hears, and He will tell you what is yet to come. He will bring glory to Me by taking from what is Mine and making it known to you. All that belongs to the Father is Mine. That is why I said the Spirit will take from what is Mine and make it known to you."

A fledgling is a young eagle that has grown its flying feathers. By now you have been going to church and have probably been going to Bible study and reading the Bible on your own as well. You probably notice new desires within you that align with the will of God. You are starting to grow and mature as a Christian, but just as in growth from a child to a teenager and a teenager to an adult, the process is long and trying at times. All growth includes growing pains; it is a process that takes time. (James 1:2-4) "Consider it pure joy, my brothers, whenever you face trials of many kinds because you know that the testing of your faith develops perseverance. Perseverance must finish its work so that you may be mature and complete, not lacking anything."

The Bible, along with the trials you will go through, will transform you into the mature Christian that God wants you to be. (II Corinthians 4:16-18) "Though outwardly we are wasting away, yet inwardly we are being renewed day by day. For our light and momentary troubles are achieving for us an eternal glory that far outweighs them all. So we fix our eyes not on what is seen, but what is unseen. For what is seen is temporary, but what is unseen is eternal." This will help you to "fly" and persevere through your trials with victory as flying feathers help the fledgling to fly. Eagles must learn to fly by observing their parents. We must do the same thing. We learn to "fly" spiritually by observing our Savior. We do this through the Word of God. (Proverbs 22:6) "Train up a child in the way he should go, and when he is old he will not depart from it." The Word of God gives us wisdom and understanding, which will give us victory as we learn from it and stand on the truths within the Word. It gives you keen eyesight, just as the eagle has. (Psalm 111:10) "The fear of the Lord is the beginning of wisdom; all who follow His precepts have good understanding. To him belongs eternal peace."

Just as God has given the eagle keen eyesight, and telescopic vision, in Christ we have this same vision, as we trust Him to lead us safely through our trials. (Psalm 4:8) "I will lie down and sleep in peace, for You alone, O Lord, make me dwell in safety." When we walk with God and place our trust in Jesus, we have peace in knowing that He is always with us and will lead us through our trials safely and in victory. But we must choose to trust Him. It is not always easy with the storms of life surging in your finances, job, and relationships, or emotional problems carried over from past hurts. As you choose to trust God and believe that whatever you go through will be for your best, you will see that God will work everything out for you. You must put feet to your faith and walk in obedience and trust. Peter would not have walked on the water to Jesus unless he first got out of the boat.

When we seek Jesus and the wisdom from above, we will find it and all the treasures it gives us. (Proverbs 2:3-6) "If you call out for insight and cry aloud for understanding, and if you look for it as for silver and search for it as for hidden treasure, then you will understand the fear of the Lord and find the knowledge of God. For the Lord gives wisdom, and from His mouth comes knowledge and understanding." (Matthew 7:7-8) "Ask and it will be given to you; seek and you will find; knock and the door will be opened to you. For everyone who asks receives; he who seeks finds; and to him who knocks, the door will be opened." As we remain in Christ and walk with God according to His will, He will light our way and illuminate every hidden truth to guide us on our way. (Matthew 10:26) "There is nothing concealed that will not be disclosed, or hidden that will not be made known."

The bald eagle, the fledgling, does not achieve independence the day it takes to the air for the first time; neither do we. Eagle parents will hover over the nest flapping their wings. Fledglings will stretch their wings for food and mimic their parents. The flapping will cause them to rise slightly. As we read the Word and put what we read into action as trials start to hit us, we will rise to new levels in our spiritual lives. Just as growing from an eaglet into a young eagle—and from a child into a young adult—takes time, so does our spiritual growth. Newly fledged eagles avoid flying over water. Instead, they keep close to the shorelines. They stay away from areas dangerous to a new fledgling.

We are to remain in Jesus always. Remain in Jesus and ask what you will and it will be yours. (John 15:7) "If you remain in Me and My Words remain in you, ask whatever you wish, and it will be given to you." So you know that He will always help you in your time of need. Stay close to Jesus and keep your eyes on Him, just as newly fledged eagles stay close to the shoreline. Jesus is our shoreline. (John 15:5) "I am the vine you are the branches. If a man remains in Me and I in him, he will bear much fruit; apart from Me you can do nothing." We cannot fight against Satan and the storms he sends our way and win. We are natural and he is not. He is out of our league on our own, but he is not out of God's. After all, God created him. (Matthew 10:24) "A student is not above his teacher, nor a servant above his master."

As trials begin and storms start to overwhelm you (and they will), remember that this is how your faith grows. When you cry out to Jesus, He comes to your rescue and helps you go through it, your faith grows, and more and more of the "world" —the impurities in your heart—is cleaned out of your heart, and more of the fruit of the Spirit grows in its place. (Psalm 9:9-10) "The Lord is a refuge for the oppressed, a stronghold in times of trouble. Those who know Your name will trust in You, for You Lord, have never forsaken those who seek You."

Bald eagles make their nests in high places, and we, as children of God, need to keep God as our high place. Even after the eaglets have started to grow feathers, the female bird shelters them. God is our shelter and will keep us from being shaken. The outcome of every situation, every trial, is always the same when you trust and obey God and make Jesus your Lord; you win. (Psalm 21:6-7) "Surely You have granted him eternal blessings and made him glad with the joy of Your presence. For the king trusts in the Lord; through the unfailing love of the Most High he will not be shaken."

Trust in God in all situations, from your biggest to your smallest problems, the outcome will always be one of victory, lessons learned, and a positive growth experience. Not only that; it is a chance to let the light of Jesus shine through you and be a witness to those around you. (II Corinthians 4:6) "For God, who said, 'Let light shine out of darkness,' made His light shine in our hearts to give us the light of the knowledge of the glory of God in the face of Christ."

Like fledglings that do not fly over dangerous areas, we shouldn't either. To us, our dangerous areas are being "yoked" together with the things of the world, or people that are of the world and have not made Jesus the Lord of their lives. (II Corinthians 6:14) "Do not be yoked together with unbelievers. For what do righteousness and wickedness have in common?" We are to leave our old life behind for that reason. (Ephesians 4:22-24) "You were taught, with regard to your former way of life, to put off your old self, which is being corrupted by its deceitful desires; to be made new in the attitude of your minds; and to put on the new self, created to be like God in true righteousness and holiness." When the Israelites married, they were to marry within the Israelites, not foreign men or women. This is not referring to nationality. It refers to their faith. When you marry an unbeliever, their worldly behaviors will make it hard for you—or worse, work its way into your heart, just as it did to them.

The foreigners that the Israelites married brought their idols into the marriage and the Israelites began to worship them. As a result, they wandered from the faith and began to disobey God and suffered due to it. (Galatians 6:7-8) "A man reaps what he sows. The one who sows to please his sinful nature, from that nature will reap destruction; the one who sows to please the Spirit, from the Spirit will reap eternal life." The lusts and sins of the world will grow like yeast and weeds in a garden and spread. (I Corinthians 5:6) "Your boasting is not good. Don't you know that a little yeast works through the whole batch of dough?" It will work itself into your life and heart and take you right back down to where you came from or worse. (Luke 11:23-26) "He who is not with Me is against Me, and he who does not gather with Me scatters. When an evil spirit comes out of a man, it goes through arid places seeking rest and does not find it. Then it says, 'I will return to the house I left.' When it arrives, it finds the house swept clean and put in order. Then it goes and takes seven other spirits more wicked than itself, and they go in and live there. And the final condition of that man is worse than the first." Why would you want that? If the fruit of the Spirit is not growing within you, Satan will not sit idly by. This is why you need to stay in the Word. It is your spiritual strength. Just as you cannot go without food or you will starve, your spirit starves as well. (John 6:47-48) "I tell you the truth; he who believes has everlasting life. I am the bread of life." He is the bread of life that will meet all of your needs whether they are spiritual, physical, or emotional. (Psalm 29:11) "The Lord gives strength to His people; the Lord blesses His people with peace."

You must allow Him and trust Him to meet those needs. He died for your freedom. This is freedom from the chains that bind your heart. He will give you peace if you not only let Him into your heart but have it and deal with the issues in it as well. (John 14:27) "Peace I leave with you; my peace I give you. I do not give to you as the world gives. Do not let your hearts be troubled and do not be afraid."

Trials are going to come, and I am not asking for more than I have to go through. When you play around with the lusts of the world, you are asking for not only more trials but trouble that could be avoided. (I John 2:15-17) "Do not love the world or anything in the world. If anyone loves the world, the love of the Father is not in him. For everything in the world—the cravings of sinful man, the lust of his eyes, and the boasting of what he has and does—comes not from the Father but from the world. The world and its desires pass away, but the man who does the will of God lives forever."

You are beginning your flight—your growth as a Christian—and just as the fledglings, stay close to your shoreline, your lifesaver, Jesus Christ. (Psalm 18:32-35) "It is God who arms me with strength and makes my way perfect. He makes my feet like the feet of a deer; He enables me to stand on the heights. He trains my hands for battle; my arms can bend a bow of bronze. You give me Your shield of victory, and Your right hand sustains me."

5

Turbulent Air

As children of God, we are not exempt from trials. If Jesus Himself was tested as described in the gospel of Matthew chapter 4, we will be tested as well. Jesus was led into the desert to be tempted by the devil. This was so He could understand the trials mankind goes through. (Hebrews 2:14) "Since the children have flesh and blood, He too shared in their humanity so that by His death He might destroy him who holds the power of death—that is, the devil." His humanity helps Him to understand our weaknesses and temptations. (Hebrews 2:17-18) "For this reason, He had to be made like His brothers in every way, in order that He might become a merciful and faithful High Priest in service to God, and that He might make atonement for the sins of the people. Because He Himself suffered when He was tempted, He is able to help those who are being tempted." We must hold on to Jesus and fight the good fight of faith. (I Timothy 6:11-12) "But you, man of God, flee from all this and pursue righteousness, godliness, faith, love, endurance, and gentleness. Fight the good fight of the faith." Your faith will be rewarded. (Hebrews 11:6) "And without faith it is impossible to please God because anyone who comes to Him must believe that He exists and that He rewards those who earnestly seek Him." God is faithful and will see you through to the end, to the day you get to heaven. (Philippians 1:6) "Being confident of this, that He who began a good work in you will carry it on to completion until the day of Christ Jesus." Even if you fail along the way, God's mercy and faithfulness never end. Praise God! (Lamentations 3:22-23) "Because of the Lord's great love we are not consumed, for His compassions never fail. They are new every morning; great is Your faithfulness."

As said before, trials mold you, help you become stronger, and weed out the impurities of your heart while helping your faith and the fruit of the Spirit to grow. Eagles as they grow older need to get rid of unnecessary things; growing new feathers helps them to renew their strength. In the same way, we need to renew our strength in the Lord daily and as we go through trials. (Galatians 5:22-23) "But the fruit of the Spirit is love, joy, peace, patience, kindness, goodness, faithfulness, gentleness and self-control." This is how in Christ we are a new creation. The fruit of His Spirit within us, and going through trials, change us into who God wants us to be. (Hebrews 10:10) "And by that will, we have been made holy through the sacrifice of the body of Jesus Christ once for all." God loves you and wants to give you every chance to go through your trials victoriously. Don't run from them; embrace them. You are promised victory! But you must run the race to win the prize! (I Corinthians 9:24-25) "Do you not know that in a race all the runners run, but only one gets the prize? Run in such a way as to get the prize. Everyone who competes in the games goes into strict training. They do it to get a crown that will not last, but we do it to get a crown that will last forever." (Hebrews 12:1-3) "Therefore, since we are surrounded by such a great cloud of witnesses, let us throw off everything that hinders and the sin that so easily entangles, and let us run with perseverance the race marked out for us. Let us fix our eyes on Jesus, the author and perfecter of our faith, who for the joy set before Him endured the cross, scorning its shame, and sat down at the right hand of the throne of God. Consider Him who endured such opposition from sinful men, so that you will not grow weary and lose heart."

Running from your problems and diving into pity parties will not help you get over your problem. Everyone has troubles. Everyone has trials. You are not alone. Pity parties only keep you in a pit of depression. Do not let your emotions consume you. You are a child of the King! Act like it! You praise God when things are going well for you. The minute something bad happens, your praise seems to disappear. Isn't God still God? Didn't He die for you? There are going to be rough times and trials in your life; even Jesus was persecuted. He is the King of Kings! Are you exempt?

These trials are for your good. They produce character and endurance. (Romans 5:3-5) "Not only so, but we also rejoice in our sufferings, because we know that suffering produces perseverance; perseverance, character; and character, hope. And hope does not disappoint us, because God has poured out His love into our hearts by the Holy Spirit, whom He has given us." When you do not face your issues, your trials and problems will not only dig the hole you are in deeper and deeper causing the sins you are committing to increase, but they will always follow you. In school, if you take a test and fail, that is it. Not with God; when you fail a test with Him, you get to take it over and over until you pass! He wants you to pass! Praise God! What a loving heavenly Father! He cares that much for you! He wants you to pass and to grow and mature as a Christian. Facing your issues, and taking them to God for help is the only way of overcoming them and getting through. (Psalm 62:8) "Trust in Him at all times, O people; pour out your hearts to Him, for God is our refuge."

The eagle will keep its feathers preened. It is important. The wind ruffles their feathers, and their feathers need to be smooth to fly properly. They use their beak to clean and smooth out their feathers. To go through your trials victoriously, you need to keep a clean and pure heart and mind. (Psalm 51:10) "Create in me a pure heart, O God, and renew a steadfast spirit within me." Initially, to be a child of God, you need to profess your faith, but along the way, we need to continually confess our sins. (Romans 10:9-10) "That if you confess with your mouth, 'Jesus is Lord,' and believe in your heart that God raised Him from the dead, you will be saved. For it is with your heart that you believe and are justified, and it is with your mouth that you confess and are saved." As we are now a new creation in Christ, we are to be holy as He is holy. This keeps Satan from having any ammunition against you as well. (Colossians 1:22) "But now He has reconciled you by Christ's physical body through death to present you holy in His sight, without blemish and free from accusation." This keeps our hearts and souls pure before God. (I John 1:9) "If we confess our sins, He is faithful and just and will forgive us our sins and purify us from all unrighteousness." The trials that you go through sanctify you day by day. With each trial you grow, and you will start to recognize after a while the things God has taught you and the impurities that He has removed from you. (I Thessalonians 5:23) "May God Himself, the God of peace, sanctify you through and through. May your whole spirit, soul, and body be kept blameless at the coming of our Lord Jesus Christ."

The bald eagle does not mate until it is five years old, but once it does, it mates for life. This is how it was always meant to be for us. (I Corinthians 7:39) "A woman is bound to her husband as long as he lives." Marriage is a representation of our relationship with Christ. Once we are His, we are His. (John 10:29) "My Father who has given them to Me, is greater than all; no one can snatch them out of my Father's hand." God never meant for men and women to divorce. That was man's initiative, not God's. (Malachi 2:16) "'I hate divorce,' says the Lord God of Israel, 'and I hate a man's covering himself with violence as well as with his garment,' says the Lord Almighty. So guard yourself in your spirit, and do not break faith." (Matthew 19:8-9) "Moses permitted you to divorce your wives because your hearts were hard. But it was not this way from the beginning. I tell you that anyone who divorces his wife, except for marital unfaithfulness, and marries another woman commits adultery."

Satan will attack you in all areas of your life. Especially in the area of your family. He wants to divide your family. Christ wants to unite it and bring reconciliation. A family together in love and unity in their faith in Jesus Christ will be strong and unbreakable.

The bald eagle prefers to ride on its back and strike with its sharp, grappling-hook talons. Anyone who is hooked by them will have great difficulty prying the eagle's claws loose. Our God is an awesome God who is strong and powerful. (Joshua 4:24) "He did this so that all the peoples of the earth might know that the hand of the Lord is powerful and so that you might always fear the Lord your God." We will go through trials so great that only God can bring us out. Jesus healed the blind and the lame as He walked the earth with His disciples, and some were just for the glory of God. (Isaiah 42:8) "I am the Lord; that is My name! I will not give My glory to another or My praise to idols." Call on Jesus in your troubles; He will always be there to get you through. (Psalm 72:4) "He will defend the afflicted among the people and save the children of the needy; He will crush the oppressor." Just as the talons (claws) of the eagle are sharp and powerful, so is our God! (Psalm 68:19) "Praise be to the Lord, to God our Savior, who daily bears our burdens." (I John 4:4) "You, dear children, are from God and have overcome them because the One who is in you is greater than the one who is in the world."

God wants your life to be a living testimony so that others may see what He has done in your life and give their lives and souls to Him as well. (Romans 12:1) "Therefore, I urge you, brothers, in view of God's mercy, to offer your bodies as living sacrifices, holy and pleasing to God— this is your spiritual act of worship."

Call on God as you go through your trials, and He will be there and get you through in a way that cannot be reversed. (Isaiah 43:13) "No one can deliver out of My hand. When I act, who can reverse it?" (Isaiah 55:11) "So is My Word that goes out from My mouth: It will not return to Me empty, but will accomplish what I desire and achieve the purpose for which I sent it."

Both eagle parents share in the caring and watching over their young. Satan will try to destroy your family and your children. He does not want them to grow up strong in the Lord. His only desire is to destroy what God loves—us—and take as many of us to hell with him as he can. (John 10:10) "The thief comes to steal, and kill and destroy; I have come that they may have life, and have it to the full." Satan wants to destroy your soul and your family, and he is the one who makes you feel dead inside and brings death to everything in your life; Jesus gives life. The eagle parents are very protective over their young and their nest, and so is our God. (Proverbs 2:7-8) "He holds victory in store for the upright; He is a shield to those whose walk is blameless, for He guards the course of the just and protects the way of His faithful ones." God knows the way that you take; He knows the trial that you are going through. (Job 23:10) "But He knows the way that I take; when He has tested me, I will come forth as gold."

The trials you go through, though very turbulent at times, will in the end help you to come through with the attitude of Christ. (Philippians 2:5) "Your attitude should be the same as that of Christ Jesus." God— just like the eagle parents—is continually watching over you. (Psalm 121:7) "The Lord will keep you from all harm—He will watch over your life; the Lord will watch over your coming and going both now and forevermore."

As the Israelites started on their way, God encouraged them by letting them know that He would always be with them. (Deuteronomy 31:6) "Be strong and courageous. Do not be afraid or terrified because of them, for the Lord your God goes with you; He will never leave you nor forsake you." Not only that, but He already knows the outcome! He has been through ahead of you. (Deuteronomy 9:3) "But be assured today that the Lord your God is the one who goes across ahead of you like a devouring fire. He will destroy them; He will subdue them before you. And you will drive them out and annihilate them quickly, as the Lord has promised." You are already assured of the outcome. You win! You need to go through trusting God, knowing that He is there as promised. In your "desert" times that even Jesus went through when you can't seem to feel God's presence, trust His Word. He will always be with you, and when you cannot carry yourself, He will carry you. Endure to the end. (Hebrews 12:7) "Endure hardship as discipline; God is treating you as sons. For what son is not disciplined by his father?" Trust Him and do not be afraid. If He would die for you, do you not think that He will protect you as well? (Romans 8:15) "For you did not receive a spirit that makes you a slave again to fear, but you received the Spirit of sonship. And by Him, we cry, *'Abba'* Father."

God gives us perfect love, and His love will never fail us. (I John 4:18)

"There is no fear in love. But perfect love drives out fear because fear has to do with punishment. The one who fears is not made perfect in love." As you call on the Lord in times of trouble, He will give you peace, a knowing deep within your heart, that tells you that He is with you and that you are safe. God gives us His Word, the Bible, to keep us strong. Whatever your circumstance, there is a verse in the Bible that will apply. Jesus was the Word who became flesh; God exalts Jesus and His Word. The Word is one of the most powerful weapons we have. (Psalm 138:2) "For You have exalted above all things Your Name and Your Word." If you read the Word every day, it will always be there to light your way. (Psalm 119:105) "Your Word is a lamp to my feet and a light for my path." (II Samuel 22:31) "As for God, His way is perfect; the Word of the Lord is flawless." If you read His Word and etch it into your mind and heart; (Colossians 3:16) "Let the Word of Christ dwell in you richly;" it will bring forth blessings to your soul and spirit. It will encourage you and pick you up when you are down. For it is the Spirit of God ministering to your spirit, through His Word. (Ephesians 6:17) "The sword of the Spirit, which is the Word of God."

God's Word not only ministers to your soul but your faith as well. (Romans 10:17) "Faith comes from hearing the message, and the message is heard through the Word of Christ." As your faith in God grows, you grow stronger as a Christian and are more able to stand against the "fiery darts" of Satan. As the turbulent storms of life hit—sometimes all at once, God will remind you of passages in the Bible that you have read and give you what you need just when you need them to give you strength to carry on in confidence. (John 14:26) "But the Counselor, the Holy Spirit, whom the Father will send in My name, will teach you all things and will remind you of everything I have said to you."

Winter is a very hazardous time for young eagles. To survive it, they must be in top condition. As children of God, we must be in top condition to go through life. Staying in God's Word will achieve this. Eagles need more than food to survive. They also need to be able to take refuge from the bitter winds. The bitter winds of life from the consequences of our own actions or the fiery darts of Satan will never overtake us as long as Jesus is our refuge and we stay feeding on His Word for our own protection and benefit. (Psalm 34:17-20) "The righteous cry out, and the Lord hears them; He delivers them from all their troubles. The Lord is close to the brokenhearted and saves those who are crushed in spirit. A righteous man may have many troubles, but the Lord delivers him from them all; He protects all His bones, and not one of them will be broken." God gives us the weapons to use, but we must use them. We must put feet to our faith. (James 2:17) "In the same way, faith by itself, if it is not accompanied by action, is dead." He gave us free will. God is a faithful God. (Psalm 145:13-16) "The Lord is faithful to all His promises and loving toward all He has made. The Lord upholds all those who fall and lifts up all who are bowed down. The eyes of all look to You, and You give them their food at the proper time. You open Your hand and satisfy the desires of every living thing." But He is also God and will not break His covenant. (Judges 2:1) "I will never break My covenant with you."

The eagles have their sharp talons and keen eyesight as weapons against their enemies. Our weapons are in God and the things He has given us. (Ephesians 6:11) "Put on the full armor of God so that you can take your stand against the devil's schemes." **The first one is Jesus.** We must be children of God to use His weapons. **The second is our faith,** "Without faith, it is impossible to please God." Your faith will get you through anything. (Luke 17:5-6) "The apostles said to the Lord, 'Increase our faith!' He replied, 'If you have faith as small as a mustard seed, you can say to this mulberry tree, 'Be uprooted and planted in the sea,' and it will obey you.'"

Your faith and trust in God will bring you peace. Where there is complete trust, there is no worry, and where there is no worry, there is peace. (Romans 15:13) "May the God of hope fill you with all joy and peace as you trust in Him, so that you may overflow with hope by the power of the Holy Spirit." As you trust in God, you will know that He will always be there to lead and guide you in all circumstances. **The third is your praise.** (Psalm 47:5) "God has ascended amid shouts of joy, the Lord amid the sounding of trumpets." If you are praising God, filling your mind and your heart with praise and thanksgiving, then Satan cannot fill it with doubt, despair, depression, and hopelessness. (Psalm 50:14-15) "Sacrifice thank offerings to God, fulfill your vows to the Most High, and call upon Me in the day of trouble; I will deliver you and you will honor Me." **The fourth is God's grace.** God's grace and His mercy and understanding will hold you up, and they are beyond our comprehension. His grace and understanding have no limit. (Psalm 147:5) "Great is our Lord and mighty in power; His understanding has no limit." When you think that you are weak and you have failed, God will always pick you up and be the strength that you do not have. (II Corinthians 12:8-10) "My grace is sufficient for you, for My power is made perfect in weakness. Therefore I will boast all the more gladly about my weaknesses, so that Christ's power may rest on me. That is why, for Christ's sake, I delight in weaknesses, in insults, in hardships, in persecutions, in difficulties. For when I am weak, then I am strong." (II Samuel 22:33) "It is God who arms me with strength and makes my way perfect." **The fifth weapon is the Word of God, the Bible.** (II Timothy 3:16-17) "All Scripture is God-breathed and is useful for teaching, rebuking, correcting and training in righteousness, so that the man of God may be thoroughly equipped for every good work." It is your encouragement, your strength, your armor and ammunition. Satan knows the Word and tries to use it against Jesus. So you must know it as well. (Matthew 4:4) "It is written: 'Man does not live by bread alone, but on every word that comes from the mouth of God.'" Jesus was the Word that became flesh. God is Spirit, and so is His Word. All he had to do was say it and it was so. (Genesis 1:3) " And God said, 'Let there be light', and there was light." God had His Word first. (John 1:1-2) "In the beginning was the Word, and the Word was with God, and the Word was God. He was with God in the beginning." The Word of God is Jesus Christ. (John 1:14) "The Word became flesh and made His dwelling among us. We have seen His glory, the glory of the One and Only, who came from the Father, full of grace and truth." God's Word, the Bible, and Jesus Christ will sustain us through life if we trust in Him. (Hebrews 1:3) "The Son is the radiance of God's glory and the exact representation of His being, sustaining all things by His powerful Word." We need God's spoken Word, His written and living Word.

(Psalm 119:9-11) "How can a young man keep his way pure? By living according to Your Word. I seek You with all my heart; do not let me stray from Your commands. I have hidden Your Word in my heart that I might not sin against You."

Our God is sovereign, and drawing near to Him in your daily walk will only bring you blessings. (Isaiah 25:8) "The Sovereign Lord will wipe away the tears from all faces." Praise God for He is a very loving God! (Psalm 112:1) "Blessed is the man who fears the Lord, who finds great delight in His commands." Reading the Word of God will keep you close to Him and keep Satan away; (Ephesians 4:27) "and do not give the devil a foothold." Reading His Word daily helps you to grow and mature as a Christian, and bring prosperity to your heart and life. (Psalm 1:1-3) "Blessed is the man who does not walk in the counsel of the wicked or stand in the way of sinners or sit in the seat of mockers. But his delight is in the law of the Lord, and on His Law he meditates day and night. He is like a tree planted by streams of water, which yields its fruit in season and whose leaf does not wither. Whatever he does prospers." God's Word will encourage you and pick you up when you are down. God's Word not only ministers to your soul, but your faith grows as well. (Romans 10:17) "Faith comes from hearing the message, and the message is heard through the Word of Christ."

There is a constant spiritual battle going on as long as Satan roams the earth. With God and His Word, you can be prepared. (Ephesians 6:12) "For our struggle is not against flesh and blood, but against the rulers, against the authorities, against the powers of this dark world and against the spiritual forces of evil in the heavenly realms." As long as you are a child of God, He will always be there to protect you. (Psalm 97:10) "Let those who love the Lord hate evil, for He guards the lives of His faithful ones and delivers them from the hand of the wicked." The Lord will strengthen you and protect you. You must remain faithful to Him, and love and trust Him even when it doesn't look like it.

The sixth weapon is constant communication with God. If you do not talk to the loved ones in your life, your relationships will suffer. So it is with your relationship with God. Talk to Him daily in prayer, and also just talk to Him as you would a friend. Pray on all occasions. (I Thessalonians 5:16-18) "Be joyful always; pray continually; give thanks in all circumstances, for this is God's will for you in Christ Jesus." Talking to God will keep you close to Him. (James 4:2) "You do not have, because you do not ask God." A close relationship with God will help you to know that He loves you and will always be there for you. (James 4:8) "Come near to God and He will come near to you."

There will be some turbulent storms throughout your life, and you will not like them, but just as clothes in a washing machine must be washed, rinsed, and go through the spin cycle to get clean, trials will cleanse our minds and our souls. You had years of the world in you when you came to Jesus. At conversion, He gives you His Holy Spirit and you become a new creation with desires to love and to please Him, but it takes time to clean the world out of you. The blood of Jesus and His Holy Spirit within us, along with the trials we go through, will cleanse us and renew our spirits. They are not fun, but once you go through them victoriously, the joy of the Lord and His blessings overwhelm you!

(Psalm 66:10-12) "For You, O God tested us; You refined us like silver. You brought us into prison and laid burdens on our backs. You let men ride over our heads; we went through fire and water, but You brought us to a place of abundance."

6

Grounded!

Young eaglets, as with any bird, need to endure a growing period and obtain their flying feathers to completely mature. By mid-June, as songbirds prepare to raise their second families, the young bald eagles are still flightless. Our growth experience as a Christian takes time through lessons learned as we go through trials. Part of going through trials is falling. The young bald eagle's flight is not perfect at first, and it will stay away from dangerous areas. Your new flight as a Christian is not always going to be smooth sailing. There will be down times when you are grounded, when your faith takes a nosedive and everything seems hopeless and as if there is no way out. But just as eagle parents will go to great means to defend their nest and their young, God will be there to pick you up. (Isaiah 41:10) "So do not fear, for I am with you; do not be dismayed, for I am your God. I will strengthen you and help you; I will uphold you with My righteous right hand." It is in those times that you truly experience the love of God and your faith grows a little more. You begin to learn through your "grounded" times, times when you fall and your heavenly Father picks you up, that God truly will be there for you always. (Psalm 145:14) "The Lord upholds all those who fall and lifts up all who are bowed down." Just as He says that He will.

It is easy to praise God and love Him in the good times when everything is going well, but true, sincere love stands the test of time and hardships. True praise and love for God come from the heart and praise God in the good and the bad times. A sacrifice of praise is praise when you are so down and depressed because of life's consequences, but you still praise God. You praise Him anyway because you know that He loves you; you praise Him because of who He is and what He has already done for you—dying on the cross. You praise Him because you believe that He said you would win and have victory. (Psalm 50:14-15) "Sacrifice thank offerings to God, fulfill your vows to the Most High, and call upon Me in the day of trouble; I will deliver you and you will honor Me."

The trials that we go through are rough at times, and just like the eagles when they try unsuccessfully to splash down and catch a fish, we do not always have a smooth flight through life, and we do not always make the right choices, but great is our Lord's mercy. (Lamentations 3:22-23) "Because of the Lord's great love we are not consumed, for His compassions never fail. They are new every morning; great is Your faithfulness."

Young eaglets get restless and while their parents are out of sight; they sleep, watch the sky or at times feel a need to exercise. As they flutter around, if the wind is high, such fluttering around may have fatal consequences. The wind may catch hold of them, and if they are not ready to fly, the wind could cause them to fall from their nest. This is how it is with us when we take our eyes off of Jesus. We tread into dangerous territory. (II Corinthians 4:18) "So we fix our eyes not on what is seen, but on what is unseen. For what is seen is temporary, but what is unseen is eternal." Even in times of seemingly complete hopelessness, we must always keep our eyes on Jesus, the "author and perfecter of our faith." If you believe and keep trusting, you will be delivered. (Hebrews 11:6) "And without faith it is impossible to please God because anyone who comes to Him must believe that He exists and that He rewards those who earnestly seek Him."

Our ways are not His ways, so we do not know how and when God will deliver us; we must trust that He will. (Mark 11:24) "Therefore I tell you, whatever you ask for in prayer, believe that you have received it, and it will be yours." Only God knows the beginning and the end of our trials, and all the in-between. Let Him lead you. (Proverbs 3:5-6) "Trust in the Lord with all your heart and lean not on your own understanding; in all your ways acknowledge Him, and He will make your paths straight." God's ways are higher than ours, and only He knows how to bring about your so that not only are you delivered, but He is glorified as well. (Isaiah 55:8-9) "'For My thoughts are not your thoughts, neither are your ways My ways,' declares the Lord. 'As the heavens are higher than the earth, so are My ways higher than your ways and My thoughts than your thoughts.'"

Life—the good and the bad times—is just how God molds us into the people He wants us to be. Only God knows the right time for your deliverance. An eaglet cannot fly until all its flying feathers are in. It must stay in the nest until the right time. It is too dangerous otherwise. So it is with our trials. (Ecclesiastes 8:6) "For there is a proper time and procedure for every matter, though a man's misery weighs heavily upon him." If you will only believe in the power of Jesus and open up to Him, He can and will bring victory to your defeats. (Romans 8:28) "And we know that in all things God works for the good of those who love Him, who have been called according to His purpose." When God is glorified, other people are affected. The Book of Daniel 3:13-30 tells of Shadrach, Meshach, and Abednego, who would not bow to the Egyptian god. The Egyptian astrologers told King Nebuchadnezzar that they would not bow down and worship their god. This infuriated the king, and he told them to bow down and worship or they would be thrown into a fiery furnace. Still refusing, they would not give in, and they trusted God to save them. (Acts 4:12) "Salvation is found in no one else, for there is no other name under heaven given to men by which we must be saved."

Jesus told Mary and Martha when Lazarus had been dead for four days to take the stones away, and if they would believe, they would see the glory of God. (John 11:40) "Did I not tell you that if you believed, you would see the glory of God?" Daniel's friends believed and they were untouched by the fire, even though the fire was seven times hotter than usual. Not only were they untouched, but Nebuchadnezzar and his officials saw a fourth man in the fire with them. It was Jesus. They were saved from the fire and promoted by the king. The king made a statement that only their God could save the way that He does. So, not only were Shadrach, Meshach, and Abednego saved and affected by their faith, but all who saw their deliverance were touched by the glory of God as well.

Satan may turn up the heat of your persecution as he did with them, but God will only allow what will turn out to help you grow and mature as a Christian, just as He did with Job. Job kept the faith, and not only were children restored to him, but his material belongings doubled! The only way to keep your faith strong is to stay in the Word. (Romans 15:4) "For everything that was written in the past was written to teach us, so that through endurance and the encouragement of the Scriptures we might have hope." As you trust in Him and the deliverance that He will bring you, He will fill your heart with peace, which also tells you that He will bring about the victory He promises you. (Romans 15:13) "May the God of hope fill you with all joy and peace as you trust in Him, so that you may overflow with hope by the power of the Holy Spirit."

Daniel's friends walked through the fire, and as promised, were saved and unharmed. Jesus was with them also, just as He promised, "I will never leave you nor forsake you." (Isaiah 43:1-3) "Fear not, For I have redeemed you; I have summoned you by name; you are Mine. When you pass through the waters, I will be with you; and when you pass through the rivers, they will not sweep over you. When you walk through the fire, you will not be burned; the flames will not set you ablaze. For I am the Lord, your God, the Holy One of Israel, your Savior."

In the Book of Ruth, Naomi, Ruth's mother-in-law, and her husband and two sons gave way to fear when a famine came to Bethlehem in Judah, and they ran. They moved to Moab. You will have times of famine when you don't feel God's presence and trouble seems to hit your relationships, your finances, and your job. These are all things to make you scared and give up your inheritance, the promises and abundance that God promises when you obey and worship Him. Fear is not from God. (II Timothy 1:7) "For God hath not given us the spirit of fear; but of power, and love, and of a sound mind."

Just as when Peter walked on water in Matthew 14:29-31 and started to fear his surroundings and started to fall, Jesus held out a hand to him. He will do the same for us. He did the same for Naomi. He did it through Ruth. You never know which people in your life are from God. You are supposed to "love your neighbor as yourself" and to "walk in love." If you obey God and walk in love, not only will you never offend anyone, but you may be entertaining and welcoming the very person God has sent to you to help in your deliverance. (Hebrews 13:1-2) "Keep on loving each other as brothers. Do not forget to entertain strangers, for by so doing some people have entertained angels without knowing it." After Naomi and her family came to Moab, her two sons married women from Moab. One of them was Ruth. After a time, Naomi's husband and her two sons died. She became bitter or was grounded. She told Ruth and Orpah, her two daughters-in-law, to go back to their own people. She had heard that things were better in Bethlehem and was going back. She had nothing left to offer them.

If you go back to your past—to your past ways—you will never embrace your future. The future that God has promised for you. (Jeremiah 29:11) "'For I know the plans I have for you,' declares the Lord, 'plans to prosper you and not to harm you, plans to give you hope and a future.'" Orpah left, but Ruth carried on, telling Orpah that she would not leave her and that Orpah's people and God would be her people and her God as well. After they came back, Ruth went to the fields of Boaz, who happened to be their kinsman-redeemer. A kinsman-redeemer is someone who takes over the responsibility of a deceased family member's property, widow, and children. In this way, they are provided for. Jesus is our kinsman-redeemer. (Psalm 55:22) "Cast your cares on the Lord and He will sustain you; He will never let the righteous fall."

So, Ruth started going behind the harvesters and gleaning the fields behind them. She picked up any grain left behind. In the end, Boaz married her, and in that way, not only was she provided for, but Naomi was, too. (Ruth 2:12) "May the Lord repay you for what you have done. May you be richly rewarded by the Lord, the God of Israel, under whose wings you have come to take refuge." God is our refuge, our provider, our Jehovah Jireh. (Psalm 46:1) "God is our refuge and strength, an ever-present help in trouble." If Naomi had insisted on Ruth's leaving, she might have missed out on the deliverance that God had in store for her through Ruth.

Remember that as new people come into your life. We must choose to place our trust in God, as He will not make us trust Him. When we do so, He will provide our needs. First, our Spiritual needs (our salvation, faith, mercy, forgiveness, compassion, and comfort) will be met. Then He provides our physical needs, our healing emotionally and physically. (Psalm 51:12) "Restore to me the joy of Your salvation and grant me a willing spirit to sustain me."

Even in times of despair when you have given way to doubt and depression, when you humble yourself and go to God in all honesty, tell Him your feelings, and ask for help, He will answer and come to your rescue. (Psalm 51:17) "The sacrifices of God are a broken spirit; a broken and contrite heart, O God, You will not despise." He provides healing to our finances and our relationships. Our physical needs also include our food, clothing, jobs, and housing. Sometimes God will send people into our lives not because they need us, but because we need them. Not because we are such a blessing; because we may be bone dry, just like the widow woman in the Book of I Kings 17:7-16. She only had one meal left for herself and her son. She was living without hope. She needed faith. But the man of God, Elijah, needed to get up off of his easy chair and think about someone other than himself. There had been a famine in the land. The people of Judah, including King Ahab and his wife Jezebel, were not obeying or worshiping God. So God sent a famine, and He sent Elijah away and provided for him, just as Jesus did for us.

But we can't expect everything to be handed to us on a silver platter. We must place others before ourselves, just as Jesus did. (Luke 6:38) "Give and it will be given to you. A good measure, pressed down, shaken together, and running over, will be poured into your lap. For with the measure you use, it will be measured to you." This can include time, money, love, comfort, or encouragement. If you need any of these, give and it will be given back to you. Whatever you give to God and others,

God will give back to you in abundance. (Galatians 6:7-8) "A man reaps what he sows. The one who sows to please his sinful nature, from that nature will reap destruction; the one who sows to please the Spirit, from the Spirit will reap eternal life."

(Romans 5:8) "But God demonstrates His own love for us in this: While we were still sinners, Christ died for us." The widow woman needed hope, food, and money, yet when the man of God came, she said she had nothing to give. But God wanted what she had, as He does with us. He wants us to surrender all. When we surrender out of our obedience and love, we have all our needs met. (Philippians 4:19) "And my God will meet all your needs according to His glorious riches in Christ Jesus." God wants to come first. (Matthew 6:33) "But seek first His kingdom and His righteousness, and all these things will be given to you as well." God must come first. The earth and all that is in it is His. (Psalm 24:1) "The earth is the Lord's, and everything in it, the world, and all who live in it; for He founded it upon the seas and established it upon the waters."

Elijah asked for something to eat. When the widow told him that she had just enough to make herself and her son something, he told her to do as she was going to do, but first bring him something. God must come first in everything. He must come first in your heart, in your family, in your money, time, worship, and praise. You should never put yourself before God. As you place God first in everything, all of your needs will be met, just as He met the widow woman's needs. She not only had enough; she had more than enough! The widow woman did not give out of the abundance of what she had. She had nothing. She gave in faith. God sustained her because she sustained the ministry. You will get your needs met by meeting the needs of others. The Lord will bless your faith and obedience. (I Kings 17:14-16) "For this is what the Lord, the God of Israel, says: 'The jar of flour will not run dry until the day the Lord gives rain on the land.' She went away and did as Elijah had told her. So there was food every day for Elijah and for the woman and her family. For the jar of flour was not used up and the jug of oil did not run dry, in keeping with the Word of the Lord spoken by Elijah."

Your issue may not be your lack of abundance or the hopelessness you feel due to this. It may be your lack of obedience in the trial you are going through. Even when harsh trials hit, we still need to obey God. In growing up, you needed to obey your parents no matter what you and your family have gone through. God is pleased with obedience. Obey His Word and His will. Put your love, trust, and faith in God. He will bless you with salvation, your home, and well-being. (Deuteronomy 7:12-13) "If you pay attention to these laws and are careful to follow them, then the Lord your God will keep His covenant of love with you as He swore to your forefathers. He will love you and bless you and increase your numbers."

Even Elijah gave way to fear. The Lord brought him back to Judah to end the rain. But God first wanted to show His glory and make Himself known to the Israelites to show them that they were not worshiping Him. They had started to worship Baal, as we often do when we take our eyes off Jesus and become too infatuated with the lusts of the world. Baal worshipers were to call on Baal to burn up an offering on an altar, and Elijah would call on God. Naturally, Baal was not a living god and nothing happened. When Elijah called, even though he soaked the wood in water to make it even harder to burn, God completely engulfed it in fire. The people repented and came back to the Lord, and then as Elijah prayed and called out to God, the rain came.

How many gods do you have in your life? What kind of natural things do you run to for your temporary peace? Temporary pleasures in immoral sex and pornography, drugs, alcohol, or even food only give temporary peace. It only lasts for the moment you are doing it. God delivers permanently! (Job 42:2) "I know that you can do all things; no plan of Yours can be thwarted."

In the Indian culture, the eagle feather is highly respected, and if for any reason the feather is dropped, it needs to be cleansed. This is how it is with us. We are going to fall at times. We are human. The storms will hit and overwhelm us at times, especially when several hit at once. We make mistakes, we shoot our mouths off in irritation, do something we shouldn't have done or fall into a deep depression. (Romans 3:23) "For all have sinned and fall short of the glory of God." God knows when you fall; He is all-knowing. Just come to Him and repent. He freely forgives. (I John 1:8-9) "If we claim to be without sin, we deceive ourselves and the truth is not in us. If we confess our sins, He is faithful and just and will forgive us our sins and purify us from all unrighteousness." Through coming to God, surrendering all, and asking His forgiveness for the sins you have committed and lived in, He will forgive. He is God; He knows all and sees all. There is nothing hidden from His sight. (Hebrews 4:13) "Nothing in all creation is hidden from God's sight. Everything is uncovered and laid bare before the eyes of Him to whom we must give account." He already knows the sins in your heart. Stop trying to bury them or deny them. We are all sinners. If you recognize this and come to Him, just like the prodigal son in Luke 15:11-32, the Lord will always be happy to welcome you back, pick you up, and put you back on the path that He has intended for you to be on.

King David experienced this. He was a man after God's heart. He loved, worshiped, and obeyed Him. (Acts 13:22) "I have found David son of Jesse man after my own heart; he will do everything I want him to do." Until one day when he gave into temptation and committed adultery with Bathsheba. He not only committed adultery, but he had her husband, who was in David's army, put on the front lines so he would be killed. That is exactly what happened. God was not happy with that. God loves us, and He loves us always. He hates the sins we commit. You may have to reap the consequences of what you have sown but don't give up. You will be restored to the path God has for you if you repent, and keep obeying and trusting God. (I Peter 5:6-7) "Humble yourselves, therefore, under God's mighty hand, that He may lift you up in due time. Cast all your anxiety on Him because He cares for you."

David had a high price to pay for his sins, and his kingdom suffered, but he did not give up. He repented and kept trusting in God. Nothing can separate you from God's love. He loves completely and forever. (Romans 8:37-39) "No, in all these things we are more than conquerors through Him who loved us. For I am convinced that neither death nor life, neither angels nor demons, neither the present nor the future, nor any powers, neither height nor depth nor anything else in all creation, will be able to separate us from the love of God that is in Christ Jesus our Lord."

You may fall from time to time and dive into a pit of depression, doubt, and fear, but trust in God's love. It is a love that is unconditional and is forever. If He would die for us while we were yet sinners, then know that there is nothing left that you could do to make Him ever stop loving you. If you sin during your grounded times, just cry out to Him and ask His forgiveness. He will forgive you and deliver you as you humble yourself and place your trust back in Him. (Psalm 34:17-20) "The righteous cry out, and the Lord hears them; He delivers them from all their troubles. The Lord is close to the brokenhearted and saves those who are crushed in spirit. A righteous man may have many troubles, but the Lord delivers him from them all; He protects all his bones, not one of them will be broken." He will heal all your hurts. He loves you. Humble yourself and repent. Come back to Him. His arms are wide open; He will forgive you and restore you. (Isaiah 55:6-7) "Seek the Lord while He may be found; call on Him while He is near. Let the wicked forsake his way and the evil man his thoughts. Let him turn to the Lord, and He will have mercy on him, and to our God, for He will freely pardon."

7

Mended Wings

In this world, you are going to go through trials. Trouble comes to everyone during his or her walk on earth. No one is exempt. The difference between how you go through each trial and the guaranteed outcome is in with **whom** you go through it. If Jesus is your Lord, you are assured an outcome of victory! (John 16:33) "I have told you these things, so that in Me you may have peace. In this world, you will have trouble. But take heart! I have overcome the world!" Even Jesus went through a time of testing. (Matthew 4:1) "Then Jesus was led by the Spirit into the desert to be tempted by the devil." Jesus had to go through tests so He could understand us as we go through them. (Hebrews 2:14) "Since the children have flesh and blood, He too shared in their humanity so that by His death He might destroy him who holds the power of death—that is, the devil." His humanity helps Him to understand our weaknesses and temptations. (Hebrews 2:17-18) "For this reason, He had to be made like His brothers in every way, in order that He might become a merciful and faithful High Priest in service to God, and that He might make atonement for the sins of the people. Because He Himself suffered when He was tempted, He is able to help those who are being tempted." Trials will come, and some will be excruciatingly painful, but take heart! In troubled times, God is our refuge! (II Samuel 22:2-4) "The Lord is my rock, my fortress, and my deliverer; My God is my rock, in whom I take refuge, my shield and the horn of my salvation. He is my stronghold, my refuge, and my Savior—from violent men You save me. I call to the Lord, who is worthy of praise, and I am saved from my enemies."

Jesus must have been weak with hunger after fasting for forty days and forty nights since He was made in human form. Satan is deceitful, and he holds no punches. He is out to destroy God's people because of His love for us. (I Peter 5:8-9) "Be self-controlled and alert. Your enemy the devil prowls around like a roaring lion looking for someone to devour. Resist him, standing firm in the faith, because you know that your brothers throughout the world are undergoing the same kind of suffering." Satan will attack you in your weakest moments. He knows your weaknesses and will use them against you over and over until you conquer them through the strength of Jesus. (Philippians 4:13) "I can do everything through Him who gives me strength."

This is why you must stay strong in the Word of God. It is your strength and your weapon against Satan. (Psalm 148:6) "May the praise of God be in their mouths and a double-edged sword in their hands." The Word is your double-edged sword, and so is praising God. If you are praising Him, then those thoughts of praise are going through your mind and entering into your heart, leaving no room for Satan and his imps to attack your mind with thoughts of depression and doubt. They are not going to stick around and hear your praises. The Word of God not only builds your faith and keeps you strong as you believe it, rely on it, and put it into practice; it is also a weapon to use against the devil. In penetrating your heart and fighting off the devil with it, it makes it a double-edged sword. (Hebrews 4:12) "For the Word of God is living and active. Sharper than any double-edged sword, it penetrates even to dividing soul and spirit, joints and marrow; it judges the thoughts and attitudes of the heart."

As you read the Word and study it you will learn God's truths and will for your life in it and God will remind you of those truths or Scriptures when you really need them. (John 14:26) "But the Counselor, the Holy Spirit, whom the Father will send in My name, will teach you all things and will remind you of everything I have said to you." You may have weaknesses, but you have Jesus as your Lord. He has understood trouble and emotional hurts and will help you through them and to overcome them. (Hebrews 4:15-16)"For we do not have a high priest who is unable to sympathize with our weaknesses, but we have One who has been tempted in every way, just as we are—yet was without sin. Let us approach the throne of grace with confidence, so that we may receive mercy and find grace to help us in our time of need."

The trials that you go through not only help you to grow as a Christian and help your faith to grow as God brings you out of them, but it is also a time for God to show Himself and to glorify Himself through you and your circumstances, and not only touch your life but those around you as well. (II Corinthians 12:8-10) "My grace is sufficient for you, for My power is made perfect in weakness.' Therefore I will boast all the more gladly about my weaknesses, so that Christ's power may rest on me. That is why, for Christ's sake, I delight in weaknesses, in insults, in hardships, in persecutions, in difficulties. For when I am weak, then I am strong." In chapter six of Daniel, Daniel was put in the lion's den for praying to God. King Darius' administrators were trying to find something wrong with Daniel, just as Satan is always trying to do with those who love the world and its pleasures more than Jesus. Satan uses these people to put God's people under a microscope so to speak and criticize the littlest thing they do to take away from all the good they do in the name of Jesus. King Darius' administrators could not find anything wrong so they got the king to issue a decree to make it unlawful for anyone to pray to any other god or man other than the king. As a result, anyone found guilty would be thrown into the lion's den.

Daniel would not compromise his beliefs and love for God to please the world. (Acts 4:19) "Judge for yourselves whether it is right in God's sight to obey you rather than God." God was pleased with that, as He is pleased with all who are His and who obey Him. He not only rescued Daniel but was also glorified in how He protected Daniel. (Daniel 6:23) "And when Daniel was lifted from the den, no wound was found on him, because he had trusted in his God." (Daniel 6:25-28) "Then King Darius wrote to all the peoples, nations and men of every language throughout the land: 'May you prosper greatly! I issue a decree that in every part of my kingdom, people must fear and reverence the God of Daniel. For He is the living God and He endures forever; His kingdom will not be destroyed, His dominion will never end. He rescues and He saves; He performs signs and wonders in the heavens and on the earth. He has rescued Daniel from the power of the lions.' So Daniel prospered during the reign of Darius and the reign of Cyrus the Persian." A lion is strong and powerful, as is Satan when matched up with you alone, but God is more powerful. All you have to do is duck!

Bow down in reverence and submission to God. You will have a strong and powerful God backing you up and always coming to your rescue! (Psalm 107:20-21) "He sent forth His word and healed them; He rescued them for the grave. Let them give thanks to the Lord for His unfailing love and His wonderful deeds for men." God may not remove you from your trial or keep you from it but trust that He will bring you through it with victory, and if you should fall along the way, as you humble yourself and call out to Him, He will pick you back up and put you back on His path again. (Psalm 18:18-19) "They confronted me in the day of my disaster, but the Lord was my support. He brought me out into a spacious place; He rescued me because He delighted in me." It doesn't matter how many times your faith takes a nosedive; as you cry out to God, He will always be there to pick you up and set you back on higher ground once again. (Psalm 145:14-16) "The Lord upholds all those who fall and lifts up all who are bowed down. The eyes of all look to You, and You give them their food at the proper time. You open Your hand and satisfy the desires of every living thing."

After feeding, bald eagles return to their roosts at night. A roost is a place where the bald eagle builds its nest. It is where it rests. When an eagle gets sick, it finds its favorite place in the mountains and waits for the rays of the sun to heal it. Just as Jesus is our healer, we can always come to Him to find refuge and strength and to heal all our diseases, whether physically, mentally, or spiritually. (Psalm 103:2-5) "Praise the Lord, O my soul, and forget not all His benefits--who forgives all your sins and heals all your diseases, who redeems your life from the pit and crowns you with love and compassion, who satisfies your desires with good things so that your youth is renewed like the eagle's."

Jesus and the Word of God are where we can always find rest. (Matthew 11:28) "Come to Me, all you who are weary and burdened, and I will give you rest." Our victory, our rest, and our salvation can only be found in Christ. Rest on Him, and He will bring you through your trials to victory and to a life of everlasting peace and joy here on earth and eternally in heaven with Him. (John 15:5) "I am the vine; you are the branches. If a man remains in Me and I in him, he will bear much fruit; apart from Me you can do nothing."

Bald eagles are attentive parents, as is our heavenly Father. He is always there for us, and in Him, we can always count on Him to help us change directions from a life of destruction to one bearing much fruit¾spiritually, emotionally, physically, and financially. (Psalm 91:1-4) "He who dwells in the shelter of the Most High will rest in the shadow of the Almighty. I will say of the Lord, 'He is my refuge and my fortress, my God, in whom I trust.' Surely He will save you from the fowler's snare and from the deadly pestilence. He will cover you with His feathers, and under His wings you will find refuge; His faithfulness will be your shield and rampart."

In II Samuel 9:1 King David is looking for someone still left in the house of Saul to be kind to: "Is there anyone still left of the house of Saul to whom I can show kindness for Jonathan's sake?" A servant of Saul, who was named Ziba, was called and he replied (II Samuel 9:3) "There is still a son of Jonathan; he is crippled in both feet." The son they are talking about is Mephibosheth. Mephibosheth, in an earlier chapter, was dropped by his nurse while they were escaping for their lives when the house of King Saul was falling.

There are going to be times when people hurt you and when your circumstances are so overwhelming, you feel like crawling into a hole and crying yourself to death. Mephibosheth was living in Lo Debar. In the dictionary, Debar means "to be kept from some right." He was living in a low place, below the place where he was meant to be. He was a prince, and as children of God, we are all royalty! (I Peter 2:9) "But you are a chosen people, a royal priesthood, a holy nation, a people belonging to God, that you may declare the praises of Him who called you out of darkness into His wonderful light." We are all princes and princesses, and we should live in a way that expresses our confidence in who we are and who we belong to. We belong to God Almighty! (Romans 8:15-17) "For you did not receive a spirit of fear, but you received the Spirit of sonship. And by Him, we cry, 'Abba, Father.' The Spirit Himself testifies with our spirit that we are God's children. Now if we are children, then we are heirs--heirs of God and co-heirs with Christ, if indeed we share in His sufferings in order that we may also share in His glory."

When you confess Jesus as Lord of your life, you become a child of God. (John 1:12-13) "Yet to all who received Him, to those who believed in His name, He gave the right to become children of God--children born not of natural descent, nor of human decision or a husband's will, but born of God." We serve a powerful and mighty God. He created the world and us; nothing is too difficult for Him. (Psalm 147:5) "Great is our Lord and mighty in power; His understanding has no limit." (Jeremiah 32:27) "I am the Lord, the God of all mankind. Is anything too hard for Me?" He is not only a mighty God, but He is also a loving God. King David wanted to show kindness to Mephibosheth for no other reason than to show him kindness and love, our God wants to show us that same kindness. (Psalm 31:19) "How great is Your goodness, which You have stored up for those who fear You, which You bestow in the sight of men on those who take refuge in You." God created us because He loves us, and He died for us for our salvation so that we would be able to spend eternity in heaven with Him. He would not do all that to let us live a miserable life here on earth.

You might have relationship problems, financial problems, and emotional problems, but as King David sought out someone from King Saul's household to be kind to, God desires to be kind to us. (Isaiah 49:13) "Shout for joy O heavens; rejoice O earth; burst into song, O mountains! For the Lord comforts His people and will have compassion on His afflicted ones." Your heavenly Father wants to mend your broken wings and restore you to your rightful place, a place of faith and rest. The trials help you grow and build your faith every time God restores and delivers you. (Isaiah 35:3-4) "Strengthen the feeble hands, steady the knees that give way; say to those with fearful hearts, 'Be strong; do not fear; your God will come, He will come with vengeance; with divine retribution, He will come to save you."

As any parent who loves their children unconditionally and only wants the best, your heavenly Father wants that for you. When your children stumble and fall, you are there to pick them up and heal their cuts and scrapes. Your heavenly Father is always there to do that very same thing to you. He longs to restore you and mend your broken wings. Call out to Him, and He will always be there to bring you back to that place of rest. The place of rest is not always free from trials, but it is a place in which you rest in Him. You trust Him to always be there for you and know beyond any doubt that He will always pick you up and restore you as you humble yourself and call on His holy name. (Psalm 80:3) "Restore us, O God; make Your face shine upon us, that we may be saved."

In the Book of Genesis, Joseph, son of Jacob, was thrown into a pit by his brothers and later sold into slavery. Out of jealousy, they originally wanted to kill him, but God's ever-watchful eye was on Joseph, and He protected Joseph through his older brother Reuben. (Psalm 121:5-8) "The Lord watches over you¾the Lord is your shade at your right hand; the sun will not harm you by day, nor the moon by night. The Lord will keep you from all harm¾He will watch over your life; the Lord will watch over you coming and going both now and forevermore."

Rueben and Judah came to Joseph's rescue, telling his brothers that they should not take Joseph's life. (Psalm 32:7) "You are my hiding place; you will protect me from trouble and surround me with songs of deliverance." As long as we live on this earth, we will have trials. People are human, and we have free will. The Holy Spirit does convict, lead, and guide, but everyone has a choice. (Jeremiah 6:16) "Stand at the crossroads and look; ask for the ancient paths, ask where the good way is, and walk in it, and you will find rest for your souls." We can choose the right way the way of obedience to God and of love¾and have life, or we can choose the wrong way, the way of disobedience and selfish gain and of hatred, the way of death. (Deuteronomy 30:19-20) "This day I call heaven and earth as witnesses against you that I have set before you life and death, blessings and curses. Now choose life, so that you and your children may live and that you may love the Lord your God, listen to His voice, and hold fast to Him. For the Lord is your life, and He will give you many years in the land He swore to give to your fathers, Abraham, Isaac, and Jacob."

When you make the wrong choice, no one else is to blame but you. When other people choose to do wrong to you, it is their choice as well, but as a child of God, you serve a mighty and loving God who will turn the bad times around and make something good out of it. Whether the grounded times of your life are from others, as with Joseph, or from your own mistakes, God is able to turn it around and make a message out of your mess. (Proverbs 16:4) "The Lord works out everything for His own ends—even the wicked for a day of disaster."

They sold Joseph for twenty pieces of silver, and our Lord was betrayed for thirty. Joseph was later wrongfully accused and imprisoned, just as Jesus was wrongfully accused, beaten beyond recognition, and was hung on a cross to die for our sins. Joseph could have grown bitter, but the rest of the story tells us he did not, and God came to his rescue. Joseph trusted in God. (Isaiah 40:31) "But those who hope in the Lord will renew their strength. They will soar on wings like eagles; they will run and not grow weary, they will walk and not be faint."

Hiding in darkness and depression does not make it go away; it only keeps you in a hole of depression, and the longer you stay there the harder it is to find your way out. Darkness is not from God. He is light. (Psalm 139:11-12) "If I say, 'Surely the darkness will hide me and the light become night around me,' even the darkness will not be dark to You; the night will shine like the day, for darkness is as light to You."

Jesus is the light; run to Him. (John 8:12) "I am the light of the world. Whoever follows Me will never walk in darkness, but will have the light of life." Joseph received a dream from God before any of this even happened letting him know the outcome. As children of God, we are royalty, and as Jesus overcame with victory when we trust in Him, our outcome is the same! We win! He even lets us know before we go through the trials to reassure us and to give us strength and faith that we will get through the rough times in life with a victorious outcome! (Isaiah 46:10) "I make known the end from the beginning, from ancient times, what is still to come. I say: My purpose will stand, and I will do all that I please."

What an awesome God we serve! Doesn't that make you want to be on His side? (Romans 8:31) "If God is for us, who can be against us?" God had a plan right from the beginning just as He had a plan for us right from the beginning. Although He knows the outcome, His plans need to be worked out through us. Trials help us to grow, mature, and learn. You learn more from experience than through someone telling you. (Ephesians 1:4-6) "For He chose us in Him before the creation of the world to be holy and blameless in His sight. In love, He predestined us to be adopted as His sons through Jesus Christ, in accordance with His pleasure and will--to the praise of His glorious grace, which He has freely given us in the One He loves." We were chosen by His grace, not by our works, to receive His grace and the gift of His salvation. (Romans 11:5-6) "So too, at the present time, there is a remnant chosen by grace. And if by grace, then it is no longer by works; if it were, grace would no longer be grace."

Through it all, Joseph did not give way to fear. Fear will keep you bound, and if you let it have a hold on you, it will keep you in the trial longer than you want to stay, and the effects that fear has on you will cause you to sin. It will cause you to do things that you do not want to do. (II Peter 2:19) "For a man is a slave to whatever has mastered him." Fear is not from God. (II Timothy 1:7) "For God hath not given us the spirit of fear; but of power, and of love, and of a sound mind." He wants you to trust in His perfect love. (I John 4:18) "There is no fear in love. But perfect love drives out fear because fear has to do with punishment. The one who fears is not made perfect in love."

As you call on the Lord in times of trouble, He will give you peace, a knowing deep within your heart, that tells you that He is with you and that you are safe. (Psalm 4:8) "I will lie down and sleep in peace, for You alone, O Lord, make me dwell in safety." God's love is so strong that He worked out salvation for us and took the punishment for us. (Isaiah 59:16-17) "He saw that there was no one, He was appalled that there was no one to intervene; so His own arm worked salvation for Him, and His own righteousness sustained Him. He put on the righteousness as His breastplate, and the helmet of salvation on His head; He put on the garments of vengeance and wrapped Himself in zeal as in a cloak." This, in fact, is the greatest showing of God's abundant love for us that He has. Calvary is all about love. A love of God the Father for us that is so great, He sacrificed His One and Only Son, Jesus Christ in order that we might be saved from sin and an eternity in hell. (Hosea 13:14) "I will ransom them from the power of the grave; I will redeem them from death. Where, O death, are your plagues? Where, O grave, is your destruction?"

God was faithful to Joseph and had a plan to deliver him. God used everything that happened as a roadmap to Joseph's restoration. (I Peter 5:10-11) "And the God of all grace, who calls you to His eternal glory in Christ, after you have suffered a little while, will Himself restore you and make you strong, firm, and steadfast. To Him be the power forever and ever. Amen."

Eagle parents are very protective over their young, as most parents are; they listen to the sound of their young eaglets crying. Your heavenly Father is always listening to your cry as well. (Psalm 34:17-19) "The righteous cry out, and the Lord hears them; He delivers them from all their troubles. The Lord is close to the brokenhearted and saves those who are crushed in spirit. A righteous man may have many troubles, but the Lord delivers him from them all." He knows just the right time to come to your rescue. As He had a plan to deliver Joseph as you trust in Him He will mend your broken heart and heal all your wounds. (Jeremiah 30:17) "But I will restore you to health and heal your wounds,' declares the Lord." Call out to God wherever you are, whatever state of mind you are in, and trust Him to deliver you. (Malachi 4:2) "But for you who revere My name, the sun of righteousness will rise with healing in its wings."

Joseph, though wrongfully imprisoned, was delivered, and was brought out into Pharaoh's palace. He was brought out to interpret Pharaoh's dreams as he interpreted two of his fellow inmates' dreams. When you witness to others, even in your darkest night, witnessing in the name of Jesus always produces fruit! Your labor is never in vain! (I Corinthians 15:58) "Always give yourselves fully to the work of the Lord, because you know that your labor in the Lord is not in vain."

It is a wonderful feeling to help someone and know that you made a difference in their life. There is no small gesture in love. One of the inmates that Joseph was imprisoned with had a dream and, Joseph interpreted it correctly. He was later released and remembered Joseph when Pharoah had a dream and was looking for someone to interpret it. He came out to interpret a dream and was promoted! He was put in charge of Pharaoh's palace! Do not despise small beginnings. (Job 8:6-7) "If you are pure and upright, even now He will restore you to Himself on your behalf and restore you to your rightful place. Your beginnings will seem humble, so prosperous will your future be."

Joseph and his brothers were not only reunited, but as Joseph forgave them and welcomed them with love, healing came to all of them, and his brothers were delivered from their jealousy. (Proverbs 10:12) "Hatred stirs up dissension, but love covers over all wrongs." Joseph acted in love and trusted in God through it all, and the outcome was total victory! (Romans 8:28) "And we know that in all things God works for the good of those who love Him, who have been called according to His purpose." Better than even Joseph imagined! (Ephesians 3:20) "Now to Him who is able to do immeasurably more than all we ask or imagine, according to His power that is at work within us, to Him be the glory in the church and in Christ Jesus throughout all generation, forever and ever! Amen."

There was another time when a man of God was imprisoned, and instead of inviting himself to a pity party, he decided to sing praises unto God instead. It produced fruit as well. It was when Paul and Silas were imprisoned for delivering a demon-possessed slave girl. The girl's owner made a lot of money off of her fortune-telling through the spirits that possessed her. Her owners were mad at Paul and Silas and brought them before the authorities with trumped-up charges.

Following God is not easy. The world is in favor of getting drunk, doing drugs, and having sex. The government even makes money off alcohol sales. Many companies make money from their advertisements with pretty women dressed in skimpy sexy outfits. If everyone would live the holy, moral lives that God calls them to, people and the government would lose a lot of money off of the drop in sales from these immoral practices.

Paul and Silas were thrown into prison. (II Peter 3:10-12) "But the day of the Lord will come like a thief. The heavens will disappear with a roar; the elements will be destroyed by fire, and the earth and everything in it will be laid bare. Since everything will be destroyed in this way, what kind of people ought you to be? You ought to live holy and godly lives as you look forward to the day of God and speed its coming." Instead of getting bitter, upset, and feeling sorry for themselves, they were singing praise to God. They were in their midnight hour, a time of darkness. The Bible tells us in Acts 16:25-30: "About midnight Paul and Silas were praying and singing hymns to God, and the other prisoners were listening to them. Suddenly there was such a violent earthquake that the foundations of the prison were shaken. At once all the prison doors flew open, and everybody's chains came loose. The jailer woke up, and when he saw the prison doors open, he drew his sword and was about to kill himself because he thought the prisoners had escaped. But Paul shouted, 'Don't harm yourself! We are all here!' The jailer called for lights, rushed in, and fell trembling before Paul and Silas. He then brought them out and asked, 'Sirs, what must I do to be saved?"

Everyone's chains came loose. The other prisoners' as well. They heard the praises of Paul and Silas. Instead of crying, they trusted in God and praised Him. The chains around them symbolize the chains around us. These chains come in different forms, such as religious persecution, financial and job trouble, family trouble, physical trouble, or emotional trouble from past or present hurts. As they praised God, it was a witness to the other prisoners who were in the same condition that Paul and Silas were. What a difference we would make to the people around us who are aware of the trials in our lives and can see the joy and peace we express. Without saying anything, our attitudes and our actions are a daily witness to those around us. They were to the other prisoners who were with Paul and Silas. Their praises brought about the presence of the Almighty! The jailor who slept through it all felt that presence and asked how to be saved. What a witness!

We can make a difference in our daily lives. The attitude you display and your actions are a bigger witness than your speech. It helps you to keep your peace and joy when you display an attitude of trust and love for God. The people around you will notice, and it will make a difference¾a difference that will produce fruit in your life, helping you to get through your trial quicker and fruit in the lives of those around you. Paul and Silas did nothing but praise God. God opened the prison doors. He will open the prison doors of your hardships and trials and set you free as well. Praising God lifts your spirit high, keeps you happy, and sets you free!

You are going to go through trials, and some will wound and overwhelm you. Trust in God's unconditional love and forgiveness. If He would send Jesus to die in your place, don't you think that just as He does not want you to suffer, He does want abundance for you? (John 10:10) "I have come that they may have life, and have it to the full."

As you go through trials and experience God's love and comfort, you can in turn express that same love and comfort and be a witness, as Joseph was, to others. You can use your trials to help you be a more loving and effective voice, hands, and feet of Jesus Christ. (II Corinthians 1:3-4) "Praise be to the God and Father of our Lord Jesus Christ, the Father of compassion and the God of all comfort, who comforts us in all our troubles so that we can comfort those in any trouble with the comfort we ourselves have received from God."

As you walk through¾not set up housekeeping in¾the valleys and trials of life, keep looking up through constant prayer, reading God's Word, and singing praises unto Him. That is your strength and your weapon against Satan's evil schemes to take your joy and keep you in a pit. If you're praising, then Satan isn't going to stick around and listen! Fill your mind with praise, and the thoughts of depression, doubt, despair, and self-pity that Satan tries to bombard you with when troubles hit will not be able to enter in. Praise God. It will help you to walk through your trials and valleys a whole lot quicker. Complaining will keep you there longer. You will stay happier, more peaceful, and in the presence of God. (Psalm 22:3 KJV) "But thou are holy, O thou that inhabitest the praises of Israel." I don't know about you, but I need that all the time. As you do this, His goodness and love will follow you everywhere.

(Psalm 23) "The Lord is my Shepherd; I shall not be in want. He makes me lie down in green pastures, He leads me beside quiet waters, and He restores my soul. He guides me in paths of righteousness for His name's sake. Even though I walk through the valley of the shadow of death, I will fear no evil, for You are with me; Your rod and Your staff; they comfort me. You prepare a table before me in the presence of my enemies. You anoint my head with oil; my cup overflows. Surely goodness and love will follow me all the days of my life, and I will dwell in the house of the Lord forever."

8

Your Flight Continues

As God mends the wings of your broken heart and lifts your faith once again, continue on and persevere. Remember Job. (James 5:10-11) "Brothers, as an example of patience in the face of suffering, take the prophets who spoke in the name of the Lord. As you know, we consider blessed those who have persevered. You have heard of Job's perseverance and have seen what the Lord finally brought about. The Lord is full of compassion and mercy."

Through the trials you go through, with each one you overcome, you begin to notice changes within yourself. That bitterness you once had toward a certain person or event is no longer there. It no longer has any hold on you, and you begin to see in the light of God's love how futile holding onto bitterness, unforgiveness, jealousy, impatience, and pain is. (Psalm 73-21-26) "When my heart was grieved and my spirit embittered, I was senseless and ignorant; I was a brute beast before You. Yet I am always with You; You hold me by my right hand. You guide me with Your counsel, and afterward, You will take me into glory. Whom have I in heaven but You? And earth has nothing I desire besides You. My flesh and my heart may fail, but God is the strength of my heart and my portion forever." After all, that is why He died to give us what we cannot attain for ourselves. (Isaiah 59:16) "He saw that there was no one, He was appalled that there was no one to intervene, so His own arm worked salvation for Him, and His own righteousness sustained Him." You begin to realize that you are growing and becoming spiritually mature. You start to see that little by little, God is ridding you of the impurities in your heart. (Matthew 15:13) "Every plant that My heavenly Father has not planted will be pulled up by the roots." The only way for God to do this is little by little through the trials that you go through. To truly be rid of them, you must see for yourself how harmful to your spirit, your emotional well-being, and your testimony those negative emotions really are. (Deuteronomy 7:22) "The Lord your God will drive out those nations before you, little by little. You will not be allowed to eliminate them all at once, or the wild animals will multiply around you."

Going through trials and realizing what God has brought you through is a part of your growth process. Continue on the path that God has marked out for you. (Hebrews 12:1-3) "Therefore, since we are surrounded by such a great cloud of witnesses, let us throw off everything that hinders and the sin that so easily entangles, and let us run with perseverance the race marked out for us. Let us fix our eyes on Jesus, the author and perfecter of our faith, who for the joy set before Him endured the cross, scorning its shame, and sat down at the right hand of the throne of God. Consider Him who endured such opposition from sinful men, so that you will not grow weary and lose heart."

As territorial as eagles are during the rest of the year, in winter, they are far less territorial. They gather in open areas near unfrozen waterways to share major food sources. Some winter grounds attract both bald and golden eagles. As adults, we think it is a sign of weakness to call upon the prayers of others, but God calls us to fellowship with others. This indeed, besides praying continually and staying in the Word, is another way that God Himself speaks to us. (Hebrews 10:25) "Let us not give up meeting together as some are in the habit of doing, but let us encourage one another—and all the more as you see the Day approaching."

The waterways are where the eagles find food. Jesus is our waterway, and we need to keep our eyes on Him always. Satan will never take a break in trying to steal your joy. We need to keep our eyes on Jesus and draw from whatever means He leads us to give us strength. As others go through trials, they can encourage us by how God brought them through, and we can receive strength from God through their victory. Then we can, in turn, do the same thing for someone else. (II Corinthians 1: 3-7) "Praise be to the God and Father of our Lord Jesus Christ, the Father of compassion and the God of all comfort, who comforts us in all our troubles so that we can comfort those in any trouble with the comfort we ourselves have received from God. For just as the sufferings of Christ flow over into our lives, so also through Christ our comfort overflows. If we are distressed, it is for your comfort and salvation; if we are comforted, it is for your comfort, which produces in you patient endurance of the same sufferings we suffer. And our hope for you is firm because we know that just as you share in our sufferings, so also you share in our comfort."

The bald eagle is not at home on the ground and we, as children of God, should not be either. We should not be at ease around carnal or worldly ways. (I John 2:15-17) "Do not love the world or anything in the world. If anyone loves the world, the love of the Father is not in him. For everything in the world¾the cravings of sinful man, the lust of his eyes, and the boasting of what he has and does¾comes not from the Father but from the world. The world and its desires pass away, but the man who does the will of God lives forever." Our high place is God Almighty. Through Jesus Christ, the Holy Spirit, fellowship with other believers, staying in the Word, and praying continually, we stay in the high place of God Almighty. (Psalm 61:2-4) "From the ends of the earth I call to You, I call as my heart grows faint; lead me to the rock that is higher than I. For You have been my refuge, a strong tower against the foe. I long to dwell in Your tent forever and take refuge in the shelter of Your wings."

As you go through your trials, do not be tempted to give in to the momentary pleasures of the world. They are temporary. (II Corinthians 4:18) "So we fix our eyes not on what is seen, but on what is unseen. For what is seen is temporary, but what is unseen is eternal." The momentary pleasures of the world come with a high price to pay. They can cause eternal damage if you let them. One thing always leads to another. Why would you want to smoke cigarettes, little round sticks of tobacco that taste and smell horrible and keep you chained to them? They come with a high price. They take your freedom. You become addicted to them. They control you. What about the temporary peace in a bottle? Liquor and beer control you as well. Alcohol distorts your mind and has caused thousands of automobile accidents and deaths. According to statistics maintained by the National Highway Traffic Safety Administration, 17,013 people were killed in drunk driving accidents in 2003-an average of one death almost every half-hour. In 2004 nearly 13,000 people died in traffic accidents involving a drunk driver with a blood alcohol content (BAC) of .08 or higher. During December 2004 a total of 1,210 people across America were killed in traffic accidents with a BAC of .01 or higher. Of those, 1,054 had a BAC level of .08 or above. In 2006 13,491 people died, and in 2007 12,998 died from alcohol related accidents. The risk of a driver being killed in a crash with a BAC of .08 is at least 11 times that of drivers without alcohol in their system. At .10 BAC, the risk is at least 29 times higher. More than 20% of alcohol-related traffic deaths involve BAC levels below .10%, so why would you want to go to something that gives you a moment of peace and most always ends in someone's death, not the death of the drunk driver, the innocent driver they hit?

Christ died to give us freedom. (Galatians 5:1) "It is for freedom that Christ has set us free. Stand firm, then, and do not let yourselves be burdened again by a yoke of slavery." Why would you want to give it away so easily for those momentary pleasures when you can go to God in prayer the Almighty God, Creator of the heavens and the earth and all that is in it, and have eternal peace? Peace that lasts forever. As you go to Him in prayer, His peace will guard your heart, telling you that it will be alright. Your prayers will be answered. (Philippians 4: 6-7) "Do not be anxious about anything, but in everything, by prayer and petition, with thanksgiving, present your requests to God. And the peace of God, which transcends all understanding, will guard your hearts and your minds in Christ Jesus."

As you go to God in prayer to help you make it through the hardships that surround you, trust Him to see you through, and you will find rest. (Psalm 91:1-4) "He who dwells in the shelter of the Most High will rest in the shadow of the Almighty. I will say of the Lord, 'He is my refuge and my fortress, my God, in whom I trust.' Surely He will save you from the fowler's snare and from the deadly pestilence. He will cover you with His feathers, and under His wings you will find refuge; His faithfulness will be your shield and rampart." Your children do not worry about where they are going to live or if you will feed them. They just trust you. We must trust God in the same way. (Matthew 18:3) "I tell you the truth, unless you change and become like little children, you will never enter the kingdom of heaven."

God warns us of the dangers of the carnal nature. (Galatians 5:19-21) "The acts of the sinful nature are obvious: sexual immorality, impurity, and debauchery; idolatry and witchcraft; hatred, discord, jealousy, fits of rage, selfish ambition, dissensions, factions, and envy; drunkenness, orgies, and the like. I warn you, as I did before, that those who live like this will not inherit the kingdom of God." The momentary pleasures of the world cannot save and deliver. Only God can do that. It is not easy, but you must persevere and hold on to the Word of God. The promises of God in it will never fail you. (Psalm 145:13) "The Lord is faithful to all His promises and loving toward all He has made." It is your weapon. (Proverbs 18:21) "The tongue has the power of life and death, and those who love it will eat its fruit." Even in your weakest moments, if you turn to God's Word, God Himself will guide you to a passage of Scripture that will pick you up and lift your spirits. He sent Jesus so we would have the Holy Spirit to guide us and help us. That is why He gave us His Word. We are fighting a spiritual battle. (II Corinthians 10:4) "The weapons we fight with are not the weapons of the world. On the contrary, they have divine power to demolish strongholds." The weapons we have are from God. (Ephesians 6:11) "Put on the full armor of God so that you can take your stand against the devil's schemes." Persevere and hold on to the Word. (James 1:12) "Blessed is the man who perseveres under trial because when he has stood the test, he will receive the crown of life that God has promised to those who love Him."

Holding on to your faith is not easy, but if you do, you will receive your promised reward, your answered prayers. (Hebrews 10:35-39) "So do not throw away your confidence; it will be richly rewarded. You need to persevere so that when you have done the will of God, you will receive what He has promised. For in just a very little while, 'He who is coming will come and will not delay. But My righteous one will live by faith. And if he shrinks back, I will not be pleased with him.' But we are not of those who shrink back and are destroyed, but of those who believe and are saved."

Bald eagle perches are usually high in the air and near water. A bald eagle can see a rabbit in a meadow almost two miles from its perch. Jesus Christ is our living water, and only through His Holy Spirit within us do we have the strength to get through anything and continue on the path laid out for us. (Philippians 4:13) "I can do everything through Him who gives me strength." Through drawing from the "living water" that comes from Jesus Christ as our Lord and Savior, you can get through the worst trial. (John 4:13-14) "Everyone who drinks this water will be thirsty again, but whoever drinks the water I give him will never thirst. Indeed, the water I give him will become in him a spring of water welling up to eternal life." (John 7:38) "If anyone is thirsty, let him come to Me and drink. Whoever believes in Me, as the Scripture has said, streams of living water will flow from within him." Look to Jesus for answers and the right paths to take, go to the Father in prayer, and wait for His answer. (Psalm 37:7-9) "Be still before the Lord and wait patiently for Him; do not fret when men succeed in their ways when they carry out their wicked schemes. Refrain from anger and turn from wrath; do not fret leads only to evil. For evil men will be cut off, but those who hope in the Lord will inherit the land." He will lead you. (Psalm 23:1-3) "The Lord is my Shepherd; I shall not be in want. He makes me lie down in green pastures, He leads me beside quiet waters, He restores my soul. He guides me in paths of righteousness for His name's sake."

Life is not easy. There will always be times of trouble. As long as Satan roams the earth, as long as we are here on Earth in our human bodies and have to deal with our carnal nature, we are going to experience trials. As children need to learn from their mistakes and the discipline of their parents to grow and mature, children of God need to learn from their trials. They help us to mature as a Christian. If God just gave us everything on a silver platter, we would never truly learn. Have you ever been around children who are never disciplined and get everything they want? They are not fun to be around, and in fact, most are spoiled little brats! So whether we are children of God or not, we are going to have trials. However, as children of God, we are guaranteed the outcome will be to our advantage. We win! (Psalm 60:12) "With God we will gain the victory, and He will trample down our enemies."

As sky-dwelling birds, it is important for eagles to keep their 7,000 feathers in prime condition. Imperfect feathers must be removed. Trials do that for us, and as David prayed in Psalm 51:10, we must also make this our prayer as well. "Create in me a pure heart O God, and renew a steadfast spirit within me." So when trials come your way, do not get discouraged. Just ask God to show you the way and to help you to understand what He is trying to teach you, or what impurities He is trying to cleanse you of. Accept what He is trying to show you, repent and obey, and move on. As you do this and truly repent, the blood of Jesus purifies you from all sin, and you will feel brand new inside with the weight of the sin you once carried gone! (I John 1:7) "But if we walk in the light, as He is in the light, we have fellowship with one another, and the blood of Jesus, His Son, purifies us from all sin."

We are to go "through the valley of the shadow of death," not build a house there! The sooner you accept God's leading and obey or repent and change the things He wants you to get rid of, the sooner you can get through your trials. Cling to God as you go through and He will help you to go through with victory. (Psalm 63:7-10) "Because You are my help, I sing in the shadow of Your wings. My soul clings to You; Your right hand upholds me. They who seek my life will be destroyed; they will go down to the depths of the earth. They will be given over to the sword and become food for the jackals."

Eagles are very protective over their young, and as our Heavenly Father, God is very protective over us. (Psalm 34:17-20) "The righteous cry out, and the Lord hears them; He delivers them from all their troubles. The Lord is close to the brokenhearted and saves those who are crushed in spirit. A righteous man may have many troubles, but the Lord delivers him from them all; He protects all his bones, not one of them will be broken."

Go to Him in prayer—trust Him to answer and take care of you. (Jeremiah 17:7-8) "But blessed is the man who trusts in the Lord, whose confidence is in Him. He will be like a tree planted by the water that sends out its roots by the stream. It does not fear when heat comes; its leaves are always green. It has no worries in a year of drought and never fails to bear fruit." When you pray for strength and guidance, don't worry or doubt that God will not help. (James 1:6-7) "But when he asks, he must believe and not doubt, because he who doubts is like a wave of the sea, blown and tossed by the wind. That man should not think he will receive anything from the Lord; he is a double-minded man, unstable in all he does." (Hebrews 11:6) "And without faith it is impossible to please God." If God who would send His only Son to die the painful death that He died for our sins, who would go through all that for **US** do you think He would let it end there? No!! (Matthew 7:7-11) "Ask and it will be given to you; seek and you will find; knock and the door will be opened to you. For everyone who asks receives; he who seeks finds; and to him who knocks, the door will be opened. Which of you, if his son asks for bread, will give him a stone? Or if he asks for a fish, will give him a snake? If you, then, though you are evil, know how to give good gifts to your children, how much more will your Father in heaven give good gifts to those who ask Him!"

Ask God to help you see and understand what He is trying to teach you through each trial. Ask for His help to get through it. Ask for His help to overcome and to continue on the flight He has planned out for you. He will help; He will answer. (I Peter 2:6) "See, I lay a stone in Zion, a chosen and precious cornerstone, and the one who trusts in Him will never be put to shame." God will never leave you nor forsake you. That is a promise! (Joshua 1:5) "No one will be able to stand up against you all the days of your life. As I was with Moses, so I will be with you; I will never leave you nor forsake you."

Each trial rids you of impurities within your heart. Just as it took years to get you to the place you were before your salvation, cleaning out the world from your mind is not an overnight process, either. Keep going through. Each trial rids you of impurities and helps to consecrate you to the Lord. (Leviticus 20:7) "Consecrate yourselves and be holy, because I am the Lord your God. Keep My decrees and follow them. I am the Lord, who makes you holy." Trials also help the fruit of the Spirit within to grow. (Galatians 5:22-23) "But the fruit of the Spirit is love, joy, peace, patience, kindness, goodness, faithfulness, gentleness and self-control." This is how in Christ we are a new creation. The fruit of His Spirit within us, and going through our trials, we are changed into who God wants us to be. (Hebrews 10:10) "And by that will, we have been made holy through the sacrifice of the body of Jesus Christ once for all." This is the process God uses to help you mature. The reward far outweighs the process. (II Peter 1:5-11) "For this very reason, make every effort to add to your faith goodness; and to goodness, knowledge; and to knowledge, self-control; and to self-control, perseverance; and to perseverance, godliness; and to godliness, brotherly kindness; and to brotherly kindness, love. For if you possess these qualities in increasing measure, they will keep you from being ineffective and unproductive in your knowledge of our Lord Jesus Christ. But if anyone does not have them, he is nearsighted and blind and has forgotten that he has been cleansed from his past sins. Therefore, my brothers, be all the more eager to make your calling and election sure. For if you do all these things, you will never fall, and you will receive a rich welcome into the eternal kingdom of our Lord and Savior Jesus Christ."

9

Your Destination Revealed!

So far in your walk with Christ, you have been through some valleys and over some mountains. You have been through smooth sailing at times, and at other times some through some very tumultuous, hurricane-force winds. Through all of this, you have grown and matured in Christ. As your children grow from babies into teenagers, you see the same in them. Sometimes they are absolute treasures, and at other times you wonder what has possessed them. Sometimes they listen, obey, and trust you, and at other times they try their hardest to disagree with everything you want them to do or at least it seems that way. You see them happy, and you see them sick and sad. You see them have a hard time at school and come home angry and upset. No matter what they go through or how hard they may try your patience, you love them all the same. As they grow and seem to understand you as a parent a little bit more and are a little less trying on your nerves, your heart just seems to smile inside. God, as our Father loves us in the same way; after all, love came from Him in the first place. (I John 4:19) "We love because He first loved us."

The eagle and its growth from an eaglet to a fledgling and into a young eagle is much like our growth. We depend on our parents for life, love, security, food, and a home. So does the eagle. The eagle is very protective over its young as we are with ours and as God is with us.

Through trials, you have learned to obey God, and it has become easier. You have grown and matured as a Christian. God has cleansed your heart of impurities through the trials you have been through. He has smoothed out rough edges that you did not know you had. (Luke 3:5-6) "Every valley shall be filled in, every mountain and hill made low. The crooked roads shall become straight, the rough ways smooth. And all mankind will see God's salvation." As well as maturing as a Christian, the fruit of the Spirit has grown within you as your worldly ways disappear more and more with each trial you overcome. In maturing, you may have noticed new passions and gifts in the Lord arise in your heart. God is starting to reveal His purpose in you. (Isaiah 46:10) "I make known the end from the beginning, from ancient times, what is still to come. I say: My purpose will stand, I will do all that I please."

As you grow and listen to your heart, this purpose will become more and more evident. God will birth desires in you as you abide in Him¾loving, trusting, and obeying Him. (Psalm 37:4) "Delight yourself in the Lord and He will give you the desires of your heart." He will give you the desires in your heart. (Psalm 20:4) "May He give you the desires of your heart and make all your plans succeed." He will also place desires there to fulfill the purpose and plans that He has for you desires to follow in the gifted areas that the Holy Spirit has deposited in you to bring glory to God. (Isaiah 42:8) "I am the Lord; that is My name! I will not give My glory to another or My praise to idols." (Romans 12:6) "We have different gifts, according to the grace given us." No matter what gifts that we are blessed with, God works in all of them. (I Corinthians 12:6-7) "There are different kinds of working, but the same God works all of them in all men. Now to each one, the manifestation of the Spirit is given for the common good." The gifts given to you upon being baptized by the Holy Spirit are for the good of all people, believers or unbelievers.

As children of God, we were all predestined according to the plan of God. That means He knows the outcome. He has been through our trials ahead of us. (Ephesians 1:11-12) "In Him we were also chosen, having been predestined according to the plan of Him who works out everything in conformity with the purpose of His will, in order that we, who were the first to hope in Christ, might be for the praise of His glory." God already had His plan for creation laid out since the beginning of time. (Ephesians 1:4-6) "For He chose us in Him before the creation of the world to be holy and blameless in His sight. In love, He predestined us to be adopted as His sons through Jesus Christ, in accordance with His pleasure and will—to the praise of His glorious grace, which He has freely given us in the One He loves." God already had a plan for creation and us.

Before God can work out His plan for you, you must answer His call. The first step is becoming a child of God. Moses answered God's call and obeyed Him, and as he did, God revealed His plan for Moses and the Israelites. Plans to deliver them from the oppression of the Egyptians and lead them to their Promised Land. (Isaiah 48:17) "This is what the Lord says—your Redeemer, the Holy One of Israel: 'I am the Lord your God, who teaches you what is best for you, who directs you in the way you should go."

As all parents want to bless their children, so does God. (Jeremiah 29:11) "For I know the plans I have for you, 'declares the Lord, 'plans to prosper you and not to harm you, plans to give you hope and a future." We need to trust God to get us to the destination that He has for us in life. He is God. He created the world and us without our help or input and He can get each of us through the storms of life to the purpose He has for us. God's purpose for each of us will come to pass (Isaiah 33:11) "But the plans of the Lord stand firm forever, the purposes of His heart through all generations." Moses had questions and was unsure of himself. He had doubts and was scared. God understood all this. He was about to be the deliverer and leader of the Israelites! What an undertaking! I would have a few questions and fears, too! God is understanding and compassionate and longs to show you His love and understanding. (Isaiah 30:18) "Yet the Lord longs to be gracious to you; He rises to show you compassion. For the Lord is a God of justice. Blessed are all who wait for Him!"

Joshua answered God's call as well and led the Israelites through many victories because he trusted and obeyed God. (Deuteronomy 31:14-17) "The Lord said to Moses, 'Now the day of your death is near.

Call Joshua and present yourselves at the Tent of Meeting, where I will commission him.' So Moses and Joshua came and presented themselves at the Tent of Meeting. Then the Lord appeared at the Tent in a pillar of cloud, and the cloud stood over the entrance to the Tent. And the Lord said to Moses: 'You are going to rest with your fathers, and these people will soon prostitute themselves to the foreign gods of the land they are entering. They will forsake Me and break the covenant I made with them. On that day I will become angry with them and forsake them; I will hide My face from them, and they will be destroyed." The Lord told Joshua to be strong, and He would be with them. This is the same command that He gives each of us. (Deuteronomy 31:23) "The Lord gave this command to Joshua son of Nun; 'Be strong and courageous, for you will bring the Israelites into the land I promised them on oath, and I Myself will be with you."

Answering the call of God and going through the trials of life to get to the destination that God has for us is not easy. They are to make us into strong warriors for God, and as our battle is against Satan and his army of fallen angels, we need the strength of God to go through them. (Ephesians 6:12) "For our struggle is not against the rulers, against the authorities, against the powers of this dark world and against the spiritual forces of evil in the heavenly realms."

Would you want your son or daughter to join one of the branches of the armed forces without any training? Would you want them to go into direct battle? No! How much more do we need the trials of life to prepare us for our destination in life that God has for us? Satan isn't going to just let God's people be victorious. Joshua never faltered in his faith as some of the others did. He entered the Promised Land whereas the others who forsook the Lord did not. (Numbers 14:30) "Not one of you will enter the land I swore with uplifted hand to make your home, except Caleb son of Jephunneh and Joshua son of Nun." (Deuteronomy 1:37-38) "Because of you the Lord became angry with me also and said, 'You shall not enter it, either. But your assistant, Joshua son of Nun, will enter it. Encourage him, because he will lead Israel to inherit it." God has plans to prosper us, and not to harm us. What glory is there for God for us to be poor and in despair? The world does not understand the Word or spiritual things. The world is carnal, and can only understand what it sees. (I Corinthians 2:14) "The man without the Spirit does not accept the things that come from the Spirit of God, for they are foolishness to him, and he cannot understand them, because they are spiritually discerned."

God says that those of us who are His hear His words and know Him. (John 8:47) "He who belongs to God hears what God says. The reason you do not hear is that you do not belong to God." The world does see the love that we show; even when we are insulted, they see forgiveness when they do not deserve it, they see the favor of God in us, as everything we touch prospers, just as it did for Jacob. Laban saw that and wanted Jacob around him. God is glorified in our prosperity and in the love that we walk in from day to day. That is a living testimony and a daily worship of God. It is not always easy. That is why God tells us ahead of time the purpose He has for us. (Isaiah 42:9) "See, the former things have taken place, and new things I declare; before they spring into being I announce them to you."

Joshua and Caleb saw the people of Canaan, but they trusted in a God that was bigger and more powerful than they were and knew that "If God be for us, who can be against us." As the crowd started to believe in the report of the 10 that spied out the land and were filled with despair, Joshua and Caleb encouraged them. They spoke out in faith, (Numbers 14:6-9) "Joshua son of Nun and Caleb son of Jephunneh, who were among those who had explored the land, tore their clothes and said to the entire Israelite assembly, 'The land we passed through and explored is exceedingly good. If the Lord is pleased with us, He will lead us into that land, a land flowing with milk and honey, and will give it to us. Only do not rebel against the Lord. And do not be afraid of the people of the land, because we will swallow them up. Their protection is gone, but the Lord is with us. Do not be afraid of them." God was with them, but due to their doubt, only Joshua and Caleb, and their family got to enter.

If God has plans for us to do something, count on Him to give us what we need to accomplish it. Faith wins victories; fear and doubt stay back in the boat and never walk on the water. God is in your faith. It comes from Him. He has given us salvation in Jesus Christ and the Holy Spirit to lead and guide us. Those are the two wings that will help us to soar! (Revelation 12:14) "The woman was given the two wings of a great eagle, so that she might fly to the place prepared for her in the desert, where she would be taken care of for a time, times and half a time, out of the serpent's reach."

To get to the purpose God has for you, you must grow. A baby is not born knowing how to walk. Babies must grow. There are different stages of life, and so it is in our Christian walk. By the time an eagle is seven weeks old, its down feathers have been replaced by flying feathers. It is no longer an eaglet, but a fledgling. It will continue to stay in the nest and grow. We do not immediately land in the destination God has for us the moment we are saved. Paul spent three years away before returning to Jerusalem to meet up with the apostles. He needed time to be alone with God. We have years of the world in us before coming to Christ. We need trials to develop us into who God wants us to be.

The mother eagle will flap her wings around her young, stirring up wind. This lifts the fledglings up. The trials and winds of life are hard and trying at times, but they will help us to soar in the end. The mother eagle will force her young out of the nest and will withhold food from them, all the while being close at hand. Her young know that they can trust her to come to their rescue. This is to get them to fly on their own. God will do the same to us when it is time for us to "fly." We can trust and have that same confidence in God. (I John 5:14-15) "This is the confidence we have in approaching God: that if we ask anything according to His will, He hears us. And if we know that He hears us—whatever we ask—we know that we have what we asked of Him."

In about 10-12 weeks, the young fledglings try to fly. This is due to watching their parents fly the mama flapping her wings and lifting them by the wind in her wings. They will not go far. They stay close to the nest. It takes four to five years after young eagles leave the nest to become an adult eagles. We are not to fear when change starts to happen in our lives and we start to get pushed by life's circumstances. We just need to get out of the boat of fear and doubt and press on in faith.

Fledglings will never fly if they do not try. But just as they stay close to home, no matter where life leads us we need to walk in the Spirit and stay close to home, close to our Father by daily devotions and reading of the Word. It is our strength that feeds our spirits and renews our minds. (Romans 12:2) "Do not conform any longer to the pattern of this world, but be transformed by the renewing of your mind."

The Word of God is His revelation of all His promises for us, and the weapon of our warfare with Satan. (Proverbs 29:18) "Where there is no revelation, the people cast off restraint; but blessed is he who keeps the law." If Jesus used it in the temptation He went through in the desert, then we know it will help us as well. God's promises are "yes" and "amen." They are eternal for us and for our children. (Deuteronomy 29:29) "The secret things belong to the Lord our God, but the things revealed belong to us and to our children forever, that we may follow all the words of this law."

God reveals His plans for us before we go into them. (Psalm 16:11) "You have made known to me the path of life; You will fill me with joy in Your presence, with Your eternal pleasures at Your right hand." The desires we start to have and personalized revelations that He gives to us before trials start to hit are to encourage us and give us hope in our trials. God has already established the work of our hands for us before we even say "yes" to Christ. (Psalm 90:17) "May the favor of the Lord our God rest upon us; establish the work of our hands for us—yes, establish the work of our hands." We are predestined in Christ and predestined to win! That was the purpose of Christ. If God did not want us to win, Christ would have never taken the punishment of our sins upon Himself. He reveals things ahead of time to let us know that He has been through our trials ahead of us, and we will get to the destination He has for us as long we trust Him. Our Father wants to equip us to go through trials with everything we need to succeed.

If God has already prepared our work for us in advance, then He also prepared the tools we need to go through the storms of life as well. (Ephesians 2:10) "For we are God's workmanship, created in Christ Jesus to do good works, which God prepared in advance for us to do." We are blessed through the victories He leads us through, and God is glorified. This is to give us hope and encouragement as we grow and are forged. Our trials will cause us to shine as the potter molds the clay into a beautiful pot. As we go through the refiner's fire trusting in God's love for us and that "He will never leave us nor forsake us," we will shine like gold and reflect His image. (II Corinthians 3:18) "And we, who with unveiled faces all reflect the Lord's glory, are being transformed into His likeness with ever-increasing glory, which comes from the Lord, who is the Spirit."

Eagles fly like hang gliders. They need plenty of open space and wind flow to obtain lift. God the Father, Jesus, His Son through whom we receive salvation, and the Holy Spirit is the wind beneath our wings. As God reveals our destiny to us, we trust Him to get us to it. God will give you the desires of your heart. (Psalm 21:2) "You have granted him the desire of his heart and have not withheld the request of his lips." He makes known to us the path of life to bless us, to give us an abundant life, and for His glory. (John 16:14-15) "He will bring glory to Me by taking from what is Mine and making it known to you. All that belongs to the Father is Mine. That is why I said the Spirit will take from what is Mine and make it known to you." He loves you so much that He gave His one and only begotten Son to die for you. God will deliver you. Call upon Him in the day of trouble, and ask for His wisdom; He gives generously, and when He is ready to move you to your destination, He will make it happen. (Isaiah 48:3) "I foretold the former things long ago, My mouth announced them and I made them known; then suddenly I acted, and they came to pass."

10

Air Attacks!

Your purpose has been revealed to you, and the gifts of the Lord within you have come alive! You are starting to realize the purpose God has for you, and you have never felt more alive than when you are operating in your gifts. You just want to explode with joy and tell the world! When you know the direction God is leading you, it gives you confidence and builds your faith and love of God even more. But do not forget what you have just come through. (I Peter 5:6-11) "Humble yourselves, therefore, under God's mighty hand, that He may lift you up in due time. Cast all your anxiety on Him because He cares for you. Be self-controlled and alert. Your enemy the devil prowls around like a roaring lion looking for someone to devour. Resist him, standing firm in the faith, because you know that your brothers throughout the world are undergoing the same kind of suffering. And the God of all grace, who called you to His eternal glory in Christ, after you have suffered a little while, will Himself restore you and make you strong, firm, and steadfast. To Him be the power forever and ever. Amen."

Satan will not sit idly by and let you just walk freely into your destiny. (Ephesians 6:11) "Put on the full armor of God so that you can take your stand against the devil's schemes." Satan's purpose is to hurt God and His people and to thwart God's purpose and plans for your life. You have been through some trials and have overcome them. Just as the Lord delivered you in them, He will keep delivering you and protecting you.

As you start to soar into new levels in your spiritual walk, beware; with new levels, there are new "devils." Fear not! Just as God delivered you before He will deliver you now. Don't forget as you start to soar to keep your eyes upon Jesus. (Hebrews 12:2-3) "Let us fix our eyes on Jesus, the author and perfecter of our faith, who for the joy set before Him endured the cross, scorning its shame, and sat down at the right hand of the throne of God. Consider Him who endured such opposition from sinful men, so that you will not grow weary and lose heart." Keep Jesus Christ-centered in your life. Knowing the direction in which God is leading you¾and as it is being fulfilled in your life will excite you and build your faith even more. But do not think for a minute that Satan is going to leave you alone. There will always be lessons to learn. We will not stop learning from God and growing in Christ until we get to heaven.

Fish are the mainstay of the eagle's diet. There are many things that are perilous to eagles. They are large birds that build their nests in the treetops. This gives them the open space needed for liftoff. Our high place is our heavenly Father. As we build our lives centered in Christ, with our daily lives as a living sacrifice to our Father, we are worshiping Him every day. We are building our lives in high places, in the shadow of God's wings, and we know that we are surrounded and protected by Him. (Psalm 17:8-9) "Keep me as the apple of Your eye; hide me in the shadow of Your wings from the wicked who assail me, from my mortal enemies who surround me."

Trials will come our way, some from Satan used to destroy us, some from consequences of our own actions, but regardless of where they come from, God will use them to cleanse and purify us. They are to change us into the image of Christ. This is much like the eagle. It has soft white down feathers as a baby eaglet, then as it grows and changes it loses its soft down feathers and starts to grow its flying feathers. The shedding of its feathers shows, and it looks nothing like the eagle that it will become.

We have a lot of the world, many carnal ways, when we are first saved, and trials are God's way of shedding the ugly and creating beauty within us. (Isaiah 61:1-3) "He has sent Me to bind up the brokenhearted, to proclaim freedom for the captives and release from darkness for the prisoners, to proclaim the year of the Lord's favor and the day of vengeance of our God, to comfort all who mourn, and provide for those who grieve in Zion—to bestow on them a crown of beauty instead of ashes, the oil of gladness instead of mourning, and a garment of praise instead of a spirit of despair."

If we persevere through and do not lose sight, blessings will come. (James 1:12) "Blessed is the man who perseveres under trial because when he has stood the test, he will receive the crown of life that God has promised to those who love Him." Like a young fledgling learning to fly, as we lean on and trust in the everlasting arms of the Lord, our trials will help us to rise high! We will rise high above our trials and walk on water in the victory of the Lord! Young eagles watch their parents flap their wings and learn from them that they can do it, too.

We have the Word, and as we obey the Word of God, we will live a blessed life. (Luke 11:28) "Blessed rather are those who hear the Word of God and obey it." Jesus was the Word who became flesh. We can read the Word and follow His example, and it will always lead us to victory. (I Peter 2:19-25) "For it is commendable if a man bears up under the pain of unjust suffering because he is conscious of God. But how is it to your credit if you receive a beating for doing wrong and endure it? But if you suffer for doing good and you endure it, this is commendable before God. To this you were called, because Christ suffered for you, leaving you an example, which you should follow in His steps. 'He committed no sin, and no deceit was found in His mouth.' When they hurled their insults at Him, He did not retaliate; when He suffered, He made no threats. Instead, He entrusted Himself to Him who judges justly. He Himself bore our sins in His body on the tree, so that we might die to sins and live for righteousness; by His wounds, you have been healed. For you were like sheep going astray, but now you have returned to the Shepherd and Overseer of your souls." As eagle parents watch over their young with their own eyes and talons, they will provide whatever is needed to protect their young; God is our Overseer and will always be there to protect us. (II Thessalonians 3:3) "But the Lord is faithful, and He will strengthen and protect you from the evil one."

Another thing that endangers the eagle is the weather. Since fish are the mainstay of their diet, when winter comes and the water freezes, it makes it very difficult for the eagle to find food. We have many things that come against us. We have family problems, financial problems, and emotional problems from past hurts, but in all of these things, we have a very loving Heavenly Father who is always there to love and to heal us; when the winter comes in our life cry out to Jesus. (Psalm 62:8) "Trust in Him at all times, O people; pour out your hearts to Him, for God is our refuge." He died to save you. He died to give you an abundant life. (John 10:10) "The thief comes only to steal and kill and destroy; I have come that they may have life, and have it to the full."

Another thing eagles have to be aware of is leaving their nest. They must always be watchful, for other eagles will come and take over their nest. If you do not abide in Christ daily, Satan will find a way to slip in and destroy your destiny. (John 15:5) "I am the vine; you are the branches, if a man remains in Me and I in him, he will bear much fruit; apart from Me you can do nothing." Eagles use their talons as weapons against their enemies. God and His Word are our weapons, and we must remember such. (Hebrews 2:1) "We must pay more careful attention, therefore, to what we have heard, so that we do not drift away." Just as not eating will make your physical body sick, not partaking in the Word of God daily will make your spirit sick and deplete your spiritual strength. (John 6:50-51) "But here is the bread that comes down from heaven, which a man may eat and not die. I am the living bread that came down from heaven. If anyone eats of this bread, he will live forever. This bread is My flesh, which I will give for the life of the world."

We can put out the Spirit's fire within us if we are not careful. (I Thessalonians 5:19) "Do not put out the Spirit's fire; do not treat prophecies with contempt." Jesus used the Word of God in His time of testing in the desert against Satan, and if it was the weapon He used and overcame by it, then by His example we should use it as well. For by our faith and the Word of God, there is no stronger weapon. (Psalm 18:30-32) "As for God, His way is perfect; the word of the Lord is flawless. He is a shield for all who take refuge in him. For who is God besides the Lord? And who is the Rock except our God? It is God who arms me with strength and makes my way perfect."

The battle we are fighting is eternal. Our home in heaven will be forever! Satan knows his destination. His pride was his destruction, and he wanted to hurt God. He does that through us. We were created for His glory. (Isaiah 43:7) "Everyone who is called by My name, whom I created for My glory, whom I formed and made." So, Satan comes against us to hurt God. Satan does not want us to get to the destiny God has for us here on earth. We each have a purpose, a destination that will be to grow the kingdom and family of God. The book of John says when we receive Jesus, we become God's children. How awesome is that!

Every time someone is saved, the angels in heaven rejoice, and it totally infuriates Satan! Satan does not play fair, and we shouldn't, either. That is why we need every strong weapon we have in the Lord. As the verse above says, "May the praise of God be in their mouths." Praise is another very powerful weapon. Instead of inviting the devil into your life by your actions of fear and doubt, resist him by faith and praise. God dwells in your faith. (Psalm 22:3) "But thou art holy, O thou that inhabitest the praises of Israel."

You realize your purpose in God now, and your destiny in Christ has come alive in you. Do not expect Satan to sit idly by and let it happen. Especially as you grow more and more spiritually and get closer and closer, to stepping into the purpose and destiny that God has for you. God had a purpose for Joseph, son of Jacob and Rachel, as we touched on earlier; he had dreams about it when he was young. At his young age, he did not realize just what God had in store for him, or enough maturity to keep the dreams to himself. His dreams were of being in a powerful position, one that was over his brothers. Because his brothers were already a little jealous of him, Joseph at his young age did not use a lot of wisdom in telling his dreams to his brothers. On the other hand, getting a revelation from God is not something you can keep quiet about. Even Jacob did not fully understand Joseph's dreams. Satan tried to destroy Joseph several times, but each time God provided a way of escape for him.

God's plan cannot be stopped. (Job 42:2) "I know that You can do all things; no plan of Yours can be thwarted." Joseph's brothers tried to kill him, but his older brothers Reuben and Judah stopped them, convincing them to throw him into a cistern, a deep tank used for storing water, and then sold him into slavery instead. God came to Joseph's rescue through Reuben and Judah. He ended up at the Potiphar's house, but as a servant of the Lord, God's favor rested on Joseph. God had a purpose and a plan for Joseph, and it could not be stopped. God blessed Joseph and protected him. Joseph found favor in the eyes of his master, the Potiphar, and was put in charge of his household. (Psalm 5:11-12) "But let all who take refuge in you be glad; let them ever sing for joy. Spread Your protection over them, that those who love Your name may rejoice in You. For surely, O Lord, You bless the righteous; You surround them with Your favor as with a shield." God not only surrounded Joseph with His protection but His favor as well. (Proverbs 16:7) "When a man's ways are pleasing to the Lord, He makes even his enemies live at peace with him." Joseph went through a lot, but he never gave up. He persevered. (James 5:10-11) "Brothers, as an example of patience in the face of suffering, take the prophets who spoke in the name of the Lord. As you know, we consider blessed those who have persevered. You have heard of Job's perseverance and have seen what the Lord finally brought about. The Lord is full of compassion and mercy."

Satan was not through yet. Joseph was accused of something that he did not do; doesn't that sound like the sinless Son of God, Jesus, who paid for our sins? Joseph was sent to prison, and this is how he ended up in Egypt. A famine was coming, and Joseph was right where God wanted him. Through this, the people would be saved from famine, the people of Egypt, and Joseph's family as well. Not only that but the broken relationships with his brothers were reconciled as well, which would not have happened if he had stayed home. You cannot walk on water if you do not get out of the boat! Satan meant something bad, but God turned it into something great! (Romans 8:28) "And we know that in all things God works for the good of those who love Him, who have been called according to His purpose."

When Joseph was put into prison, he interpreted some dreams for two of the prisoners, and both came true. This in turn led him to interpret two of Pharaoh's dreams, which were given by God. Joseph's steps were directed by God all along. (Proverbs 20:24) "A man's steps are directed by the Lord. How then can anyone understand his own way." Joseph interpreted correctly and was put in charge of Pharaoh's palace. There was no one in all of Egypt, except Pharaoh himself, higher in authority than Joseph. The dreams Joseph had as a boy did come true. He did not give up, and his dreams came true. The dreams Pharaoh had were of seven years of plenty and seven years of famine. Through the wisdom that God gave Joseph, he had a plan to prepare for the years of famine. This is what led his family to Egypt and eventually to meet up and reunite with Joseph. Joseph persevered and trusted in God, and he was rewarded. He stepped into his destiny. We can, too, if we do not give up. We have to fight with weapons of faith: the Word, perseverance, and praise, for the name of Judah means praise. (II Corinthians 10:4) "The weapons we fight with are not the weapons of the world. On the contrary, they have divine power to demolish strongholds." The weapons we have are from God. (Ephesians 6:11) "Put on the full armor of God so that you can take your stand against the devil's schemes." God hears our call and will "never leave us nor forsake us." He is always faithful. (Daniel 10:12) "Do not be afraid, Daniel. Since the first day that you set your mind to gain understanding and to humble yourself before your God, your words were heard, and I have come in response to them"

Nehemiah was another who persevered and overcame. He accomplished the task God had for him. The Israelites had been exiled. The walls of Jerusalem and the temple of the Lord had been destroyed when the Egyptians took them captive. The walls broken down were a symbol of the state of their relationship with God. The Israelites followed after other gods too many times and turned their backs on God. They reaped the consequences of their own actions. But God, being a loving and forgiving God, did not give up on them. He already had people in mind to restore the wall and the temple. Nehemiah went to Jerusalem and was distraught at the condition of the wall. He was only a cupbearer to the king and was afraid to ask the king to go to Jerusalem to restore it, but he prayed to God and asked forgiveness on behalf of the Israelites. Afraid, he went to the king and asked to go. God always hears the prayers of His children. (Psalm 145:148-19) "The Lord is near to all who call on Him, to all who call on Him in truth. He fulfills the desires of those who fear Him; He hears their cry and saves them." The king not only let him go, but he sent provisions with him. That is God!

Nehemiah did not give into fear. He overcame it. The Lord has plans for you and will make provisions for them to be accomplished. Nehemiah was not without opposition. He had people to help, and he positioned them in different places to accomplish the task. Satan did not want Nehemiah to succeed. Satan rallied people to oppose him and try to stop the building. He did not succeed. Nehemiah did not become weary or give in to the tactics of the devil, and the wall was built.

The wall broken down was a symbol of the broken relationship between the Israelites and God. The repairing of the wall and its completion was a symbol of their restored relationship with God and His wall of protection. That wall of protection is there for us. The different gates of the wall represent Christ the Valley Gate, which brings us to humility to repent; the Dung Gate, which is the cleansing of our souls through belief in Him admitting our sins, asking forgiveness, and receiving Him; the Fountain Gate, which is His Holy Spirit being poured into us and within that the wall of the Pool of Siloam, which is the healing power of God through the Holy Spirit; the Fish Gate, which is God's constant provision whether it is physical, spiritual, emotional or mental, and the call we each have to be "Fishers of Men;" the Water Gate, which is the Holy Spirit and the Word, our sword of protection, a weapon against Satan, and our bread for our spiritual nourishment; and the Horse Gate, which is spiritual warfare. God has given us everything we need to walk in and through our destiny and the fiery darts Satan gives us. (Hebrews 13:20-21) "That great Shepherd of the sheep, equip you with everything good for doing His will, and may He work in us what is pleasing to Him, through Jesus Christ, to whom be glory forever and ever. Amen." He gives us everything we need to fight the battle, for the battle belongs to Him. He has given everyone a measure of faith in which faith as small as a mustard seed can move a mountain. He has given us His Spirit within us, and His Word, which is "sharper than any double-edged sword." God has laid a plan for our redemption since the beginning of time, and He has a plan for every one of us. We all play a part in it. If you do not get weary and give up, you will reach your destiny as well and walk in victory just as Joseph and Nehemiah did. (Galatians 6:9) "Let us not become weary in doing good, for at the proper time we will reap a harvest if we do not give up."

11

ᵔᵔ

Continue Your Flight! Victory is Promised!

You are almost there! You have noticed things within yourself that God has changed. You are seeing God's plan being laid out before you, just like Nehemiah as he neared the finish line. Can you imagine the joy he felt as he and the other Israelites who continued and saw the completion of the wall through, as they put up the final portion of the last wall? Victory is ours. It is promised and God is faithful to all His promises. (Psalm 60:12) "With God we will gain the victory, and He will trample down our enemies."

As a bird that is meant to soar will die on the ground, if we do not rise above our circumstances, if we keep giving in to the carnal nature within us, we will never get out of the boat of familiarity and fly on the wings of an eagle, on the wings of our God. The carnal nature within us wars against the spirit; it wants comfort. If the young fledgling never tried to flap its wings and fly, it would never get out of the nest. When an eagle is about to die, it returns to its favorite place. Our favorite place should be in Christ, as we should die daily to self, carrying our cross and living spirit-filled lives for Christ. (Luke 9:23-26) "If anyone would come after Me, he must deny himself and take up his cross daily and follow Me. For

98

whoever wants to save his life will lose it, but whoever loses his life for Me will save it. What good is it for a man to gain the whole world, and yet lose or forfeit his very self? If anyone is ashamed of Me and My words, the Son of Man will be ashamed of him when He comes in His glory and in the glory of the Father and of the holy angels." If we make the choice to die to self daily, then it will not be us that shines; it will be Jesus Christ shining through us.

Only in Christ can we overcome and continue to walk through victoriously. You are in the beginning stages of seeing God's plan for you being birthed. Satan will never stop trying to destroy your walk and your testimony. You are saved, and that cannot be changed, but your testimony can win many others to Christ, and that is what Satan wants stopped. You must continue in the Word and stand strong. (II Thessalonians 2:14-15) "God chose you to be saved through the sanctifying work of the Spirit and through belief in the truth. He called you to this through our gospel, that you might share in the glory of our Lord Jesus Christ. So then, brothers, stand firm and hold to the teachings we passed on to you, whether by word of mouth or by letter." You are a saved, born-again child of God, and your destiny is coming alive in you, but you are still flesh. Satan will try to use the same things on you that kept you away from God to start with. (Galatians 5:16-17) "So I say, live by the Spirit, and you will not gratify the desires of the sinful nature. For the sinful nature desires what is contrary to the Spirit and the Spirit what is contrary to the sinful nature." This is the only way for us to control our emotions instead of letting our emotions control us. (II Peter 2:19) "For a man is a slave to whatever has mastered him."

If you live in the Spirit, you will want to meditate on the Word of God, which is your strength, to live a holy life. Without it, you will fall. (Joshua 1:8) "Do not let this Book of the Law depart from your mouth; meditate on it day and night, so that you may be careful to do everything written in it. Then you will be prosperous and successful." Doing this will transform your mind into agreement with the will of God. (Romans 12:2) "Do not conform any longer to the patterns of this world, but be transformed by the renewing of your mind. Then you will be able to test and approve what God's will is His good, pleasing and perfect will."

As you meditate on the Word and trials that come your way, no matter what your emotions may dictate to you, you will know the promises and will of God. If you walk in the Spirit, you will stand on those promises. Only by standing on those promises will you be victorious. (Isaiah 7:9) "If you do not stand firm in your faith, you will not stand at all."

I have seen so many Christians fall away due to hardships of life, and Satan, knowing their weaknesses, dangles them before them. If you do not stay spiritually fed every day by the Word and your own devotion time with God, your spirit will get weak. Remember that when hardships and sudden disasters come, Satan loves to take advantage of weakness and dangles it in front of you. Do not consider yourself out of Satan's reach just because you are walking into your destiny. Beware! This is when Satan will fight his hardest! (I Corinthians 16:13) "Be on your guard, stand firm in the faith; be men of courage; be strong. Do everything in love." When an Indian receives an Eagle feather, he is being given ultimate respect, gratitude, and love. The one that holds the feather must keep that respect. It is considered sacred. He must never contaminate or change his state of mind. (Psalm 51:10-12) "Create in me a pure heart, O God, and renew a steadfast spirit within me. Do not cast me from Your presence or take Your Holy Spirit from me. Restore to me the joy of Your salvation and grant me a willing spirit, to sustain me." As children of God filled with the Holy Spirit, we are to live holy lives. (Philippians 4:11-13) "For I have learned to be content whatever the circumstances. I know what it is to be in need, and I know what it is to have plenty. I have learned the secret of being content in any and every situation, whether well-fed or hungry, whether living in plenty or in want. I can do everything through Him who gives me strength."

We cannot do this on our own. We rely on the power and the strength of the Holy Spirit, but the choice to obey the leading and voice of the Holy Spirit is still ours. (II Corinthians 6:14) "Do not be yoked together with unbelievers. For what do righteousness and wickedness have in common?" (II Corinthians 6:17) "Therefore come out from them and be separate, says the Lord. Touch no unclean thing, and I will receive you." We are to do this by receiving forgiveness for our sins. God is holy and we are to be holy. (I Peter 1:16) "Be holy, because I am holy." When you leave a life of sin, you are not to bring anything to cause you to sin into your household. The battle we fight is really a fight between God and Satan. It started ages ago when Satan's pride got the best of him and he rebelled against God. We are caught in the middle, but as long as we hold fast to the Lord and let the Holy Spirit work through us, our battle will always be one of victory, and we will spend eternity in heaven with the Father away from the pain and suffering we experience from time to time here on earth. (Exodus 14:13-14) "Do not be afraid. Stand firm and you will see the deliverance the Lord will bring you today. The Egyptians you see today you will never see again. The Lord will fight for you; you need only to be still." This means to trust in the love and faithfulness of our God. (John 3:16) "For God so loved the world that He gave His One and only Son, that whoever believes in Him shall not perish but have eternal life." I say it is more than worth it! Look at what Jesus did for us. (Colossians 2:13-15) "When you were dead in your sins and in the uncircumcision of your sinful nature, God made you alive with Christ. He forgave us all our sins, having canceled the written code, with its regulations, that was against us and that stood opposed to us. He took it away, nailing it to the cross. Having disarmed the powers and authorities, He made a public spectacle of them, triumphing over them by the cross."

Fledged eaglets do not fish for themselves for at least a month after they leave the nest. They return home to eat food delivered by their parents. We, as Christians who are carnal and natural, cannot expect to fight a spiritual battle on our own. Evil has come to the whole world and will fall on every man. Satan is not going to leave anyone alone or untouched by his fiery darts. Jesus is the bread of life and we need Him, the Holy Spirit, and God's Word every day that we are alive here on the earth. Even walking in your destiny¾whether God has called you to sing, to be in the ministry, to be a Sunday school teacher, to work a secular job and witness daily to your coworkers living a daily sacrifice to God, you will always need to feed on God's Holy Word. (John 6:35) "I am the bread of life. He who comes to Me will never go hungry, and he who believes in Me will never be thirsty."

God knows that we are but flesh, and He made allowances for us when we fall. That is why Jesus Christ's arms were wide open. He allowed for past, present, and future forgiveness. Great is God's faithfulness. (Psalm 145:14) "The Lord upholds all those who fall and lifts up all those who are bowed down." All you have to do is humble yourself and repent. You do have a choice daily, and if you keep giving in to your flesh, you will die spiritually, quenching the fire of the Holy Spirit more and more each day. Take the man that lived in the tombs; he lived around dead people! (Mark 5:1-3) "They went across the lake to the region of the Gerasenes. When Jesus got out of the boat, a man with an evil spirit came from the tombs to meet him. This man lived in the tombs, and no one could bind him anymore, not even with a chain." Do you want life, and life more abundantly? Temptations will come, but so will a way of escape provided by the Father. (I Corinthians 10:12-13) "So, if you think you are standing firm, be careful that you don't fall! No temptation has seized you except what is common to man. And God is faithful; He will not let you be tempted beyond what you can bear. But when you are tempted, He will also provide a way out so that you can stand up under it." You need only to heed His warning and obey. God's grace is never-ending. He loves you. That is why He sent Jesus. (Lamentations 3:22-23) "Because of the Lord's great love we are not consumed, for His compassions never fail. They are new every morning; great is Your faithfulness."

The eagle's tail feathers stabilize the eagle for easier landing and maneuvering. That is what our Lord is for us. His Spirit within us, and staying in His Word daily keeps us stable and strong spiritually. It is ok to have desires. God even says that He will "give you the desires of your heart." What counts is the attitude of your heart. It can overtake you. (Romans 12:21) "Do not be overcome by evil, but overcome evil with good." New life bursts forth as you die to self, to the "I want"s, and to the "what about me"s. If you let that consume you, it becomes selfishness and pride. If you give in to that, you will never experience all God has for you. You must "go forth," continue on the course God has for you, and walk through the valleys of life in victory. (Psalm 23:1-4) "The Lord is my Shepherd, I shall not be in want. He makes me lie down in green pastures, He leads me beside quiet waters, He restores my soul. He guides me in paths of righteousness for His name's sake. Even though I walk through the valley of the shadow of death, I will fear no evil, for You are with me; Your rod and Your staff; they comfort me." In doing this, you shed self and gain Christ. (Philippians 1:21) "For to me, to live is Christ and to die is gain." Unless you die to the flesh that wants to rise up, consume you, and cause you to walk contrary to the Spirit, you will end up like the man in the tombs instead of the "Eagle's Flight" that God has for you.

If Satan knocks you down, get up! You do not have to stay that way! Victory is already promised to you! (I Corinthians 15:54-58) "Death has been swallowed up in victory. Where, O death, is your victory? Where, O death, is your sting? The sting of death is sin, and the power of sin is the law. But thanks be to God! He gives us the victory through our Lord Jesus Christ. Therefore, my dear brothers, stand firm. Let nothing move you. Always give yourselves fully to the work of the Lord, because you know that your labor in the Lord is not in vain." Jesus walked through the Kidron Valley, the valley of death. He walked through dying on the cross, and on to His resurrection and our victory! (John 18:1) "When He had finished praying, Jesus left with His disciples and crossed the Kidron Valley. On the other side, there was an olive grove and He and His disciples went into it." The olive grove is a symbol of the Holy Spirit and of victory! Satan will not give up, but what shows your maturity in Christ is how you handle the fiery darts Satan throws at you. Your heavenly Father gives you the strength to stand firm in your faith. (II Corinthians 1:21-23) "Now it is God who makes both us and you stand firm in Christ. He anointed us, set His seal of ownership on us, and put His Spirit in our hearts as a deposit, guaranteeing what is to come. I call God as my witness that it was in order to spare you that I did not return to Corinth. Not that we lord it over your faith, but we work with you for your joy, because it is by faith you stand firm." The power of the resurrection is in knowing and believing in and receiving God's never-ending grace, forgiveness, and love. (John 15:13) "Greater love has no one than this, that he lay down his life for his friends."

So, as children of God, it doesn't matter what you are called to do, just remember who you are in Christ, and whose you are. Knowing who you are in Christ and the extent of His love will give you the strength and confidence to face anything because you know who you belong to and who your big Brother is. (II Corinthians 5:14-15) "For Christ's love compels us, because we are convinced that one died for all, and therefore all died. And He died for all, that those who live should no longer liver for themselves but for Him who died for them and was raised again." You are a child of the Most High God! Satan cannot take that away. He just tries to make you doubt that when you mess up, but "great is thy faithfulness." Just continue your flight. (Colossians 1:21-23) "Once you were alienated from God and were enemies in your minds because of your evil behavior. But now He has reconciled you by Christ's physical body through death to present you holy in His sight, without blemish and free from accusation—if you continue in your faith established and firm, not moved from the hope held out in the gospel."

Eagle feathers were given to Indian braves for tremendous acts of bravery. These feathers were very difficult to come by and were earned one at a time. God does not expect you to stand against the hardships of life on your own. He knows "apart from Me you can do nothing." That is why He sent Jesus, and His Holy Spirit gives us the boldness to do the Lord's work and live for Him. (Acts 4:29) "Now, Lord, consider their threats and enable Your servants to speak Your Word with great boldness." The bravery God asks of us is to live for Christ, and that is not always easy. Jesus was beaten beyond human recognition, was hung on a cross, died, and rose from the dead all for us. (Mark 9:31) "The Son of Man is going to be betrayed into the hands of men. They will kill Him, and after three days He will rise again."

We may not be asked to physically die on a cross, but we can humbly accept the path God has laid out for us and "go forth" to continue our walk in Christ with the daily ups and downs. As long as we are on earth and Satan is alive and kicking, we are going to have hardships. Walking in your destiny is not the end of Satan's attacks. Continue your flight, but do it guarded. Be alert, not afraid, and continue in the joy of the Lord. (James 5:8) "You too, be patient and stand firm, because the Lord's coming is near. Don't grumble against each other, brothers, or you will be judged. The Judge is standing at the door!"

Enjoy¾you're the path God is leading you on. Trust that He is always watching over you. Continue your flight. But never let your head get so caught up in the clouds that you forget about Satan, or he will catch you off your guard. Do not walk around in fear every moment; just be strong in the Lord. If you walk in His love and in His Word daily, He will always be your rear guard. (Isaiah 58:6-11) "Is not this the kind of fasting I have chosen; to loose the chains of injustice and untie the cords of the yoke, to set the oppressed free and break every yoke? Is it not to share your food with the hungry and to provide the poor wanderer with shelter—when you see the naked, to clothe him, and not to turn away from your own flesh and blood? Then your light will break forth like the dawn, and your healing will quickly appear; then your righteousness will go before you, and the glory of the Lord will be your rear guard. Then you will call, and the Lord will answer; you will cry for help, and He will say; Here am I. If you do away with oppression, with the pointing fingers and malicious talk, and if you spend yourselves on behalf of the hungry and satisfy the needs of the oppressed, then your light will rise in the darkness, and your night will become like the noonday. The Lord will guide you always; He will satisfy your needs in a sun-scorched land and will strengthen your frame. You will be like a well-watered garden, like a spring whose waters never fail."

12

A Young Eagle

Is your spirit bursting with joy as you walk out of the destination that God has laid out before you? You have learned to trust God. You have been through some extremely harsh times and thought that you would never make it. (Acts 14: 22-23) "We must go through many hardships to enter the kingdom of God,' they said. Paul and Barnabas appointed elders for them in each church and, with prayer and fasting, committed them to the Lord, in whom they had put their trust." You have cried, despaired, and wanted to end it all, and then God shows up and gives you hope, and picks you up again. You have finally learned to trust in His never-ending love and faithfulness. (Psalm 9:10) "Those who know Your name will trust in You, for You Lord, have never forsaken those who seek You." He has always been there for you. He has revealed qualities in you that need to be changed into the likeness of Christ. He has also given you revelations of things to come that have helped you and given you hope to carry on. Though God has given you revelations at times through His Word, a dream, or just a knowing deep in your heart, you have often wondered why He doesn't always make His revelations a little bit clearer. First of all, that is in part because He is God and He does not have to clear His plans with you first¾just as you don't always tell your children every little detail. Quite often I am sure when they ask why they have to do something, you say, "Because I said so!" Well, God, being our Father, does the same, but He also holds things out due to the fact that Satan cannot read your mind, but He can hear! God's plan cannot be thwarted, but Satan can hold it up! (I Thessalonians 2:18) "For we wanted to come to you—certainly I, Paul, did again and again—but Satan stopped us." We can be our own worst enemy by giving in to our flesh, but Satan is worse. God wants to bless us, not hinder us. So, at times, when He does not always make everything crystal clear, remember it is for your good. The secret things really do belong to God. (Deuteronomy 29:29) "The secret things belong to the Lord our God, but the things revealed belong to us and to our children forever, that we may follow all the words of this law." God gave us His Word, and if it was powerful enough for Him when He created the world, it is good enough for us to use to keep us strong and to use against all the devil's schemes.

You are stronger, not fearful; you have become more loving and gentle. You are showing more of the character of Christ. (II Corinthians 3:17-18) "Now the Lord is the Spirit, and where the Spirit of the Lord is, there is freedom. Ad we, who with unveiled faces all reflect the Lord's glory, are being transformed into His likeness with ever-increasing glory, which comes from the Lord, who is the Spirit."

When we are first saved, we have a lot of the world in us and are completely different after years of walking faithfully in Christ. (Colossians 3:12-17) "Therefore, as God's chosen people, holy and dearly loved, clothe yourselves with compassion, kindness, humility, gentleness, and patience. Bear with each other and forgive whatever grievances you may have against one another. Forgive as the Lord forgave you. And over all these virtues put on love, which binds them all together in perfect unity. Let the peace of Christ rule in your hearts, since as members of one body you were called to peace. And be thankful. Let the word of Christ dwell in you richly as you teach and admonish one another with all wisdom, and as you sing psalms, hymns, and spiritual songs with gratitude in your hearts to God. And whatever you do, whether in word or deed, do it all in the name of the Lord Jesus, giving thanks to God the Father through Him."

The bald eagle has a distinctive white head and tail feathers. They do not appear until the bald eagle is about four to five years old. As we grow and mature in Christ, we become more and more like Him. (James 1:2-5) "Consider it pure joy, my brothers, whenever you face trials of many kinds because you know that the testing of your faith develops perseverance. Perseverance must finish its work so that you may be mature and complete, not lacking anything. If any of you lacks wisdom, he should ask God, who gives generously to all without finding fault, and it will be given to him." It is through the trials that we have gone through that we are changed into the image of Christ. (Philippians 2:5) "Your attitude should be the same as that of Christ Jesus." It was not always easy, but you have found that as you took each step of saying "no" to ungodliness and to the flesh, and everything that is not Christlike, with the help of the Holy Spirit, it became easier and easier. Eagles are made to fly in high places. So are we. We are created in the image of God, and as we entrust ourselves to Him, He will help us to soar and overcome. He keeps us in peace. (Isaiah 26:3) "You will keep in perfect peace him whose mind is steadfast because he trusts in You."

The trials that you have gone through and will go through have helped you to mature in Christ. We will not be perfect until we reach heaven, because we are flesh. But the Holy Spirit will help you to "imitate Christ." (Ephesians 5:1) "Be imitators of God, therefore, as dearly loved children and live a life of love, just as Christ loved us and gave Himself up for us as a fragrant offering and sacrifice to God." You have learned to lean on Christ. (Psalm 28:8-9) "The Lord is the strength of His people, a fortress of salvation for His anointed one. Save Your people and bless Your inheritance; be their Shepherd and carry them forever." The eagle has now become an adult eagle, and since it has first taken flight, has changed a lot. Much like us. It uses its broad wings to glide and relies on air currents to help it to float on the air stream. It helps the eagle to save energy and glide on the wind for hours without flapping its wings. That is much like our heavenly Father. When we learn to trust Him, He holds us up. (Psalm 37:23-25) "If the Lord delights in a man's way, He makes his steps firm; though he stumbles, he will not fall, for the Lord upholds him with His hand. I was young and now I am old, yet I have never seen the righteous forsaken or their children begging bread." As you have grown and matured spiritually, you have experienced this for yourself. You probably want to kick yourself for all the crying you did in the past out of fear of the "unknown," and wish that you would have just trusted God! (I John 4:17-18) "There is no fear in love. But perfect love drives out fear because fear has to do with punishment. The one who fears is not made perfect in love." Trusting in God keeps you happy. I like that a whole lot more. Having matured in your Christian walk, people who know you notice the changes in you as if you now shine! This is something that as a child of God, we should all want. The strongest testimony we have is our daily life. (II Corinthians 4:6) "For God, who said, 'Let light shine out of darkness,' made His light shine in our hearts to give us the light of the knowledge of the glory of God in the face of Christ."

When first out of the nest, a young bald eagle is glossy black, but as it matures, it dramatically changes and has a mix of brown and white feathers. It takes time for it to mature. Just as a child grows from a baby to a child to a teenager, then a young adult, and finally to maturity! Most of us who have children know it is by the grace of God that we made it through their growth period. As a mature Christian, never forget where you came from and the lack of patience you once had. This has only been somewhat perfected through the tests and trials that you have been through. You are not done learning yet, and there are probably still more things that God wants to teach you and weed out of you. Remembering where you came from helps you to truly walk in the Spirit and treat others with the patience and understanding you wanted as you went through your spiritual puberty phase. We grow from glory to glory, changing more and more into the likeness of Jesus Christ. Your character has changed dramatically as well. (Galatians 3:26-28) "You are all sons of God through faith in Christ Jesus, for all of you who were baptized into Christ have clothed yourselves with Christ." If you once got drunk and high, you no longer do that. God keeps you in peace. (Psalm 29:11) "The Lord gives strength to His people; the Lord blesses His people with peace." If you once had a problem with your temper or were extremely prideful and selfish, the power of the Holy Spirit has tamed you. The Holy Spirit is powerful, and as the bald eagle changes dramatically from an eaglet to an adult eagle, the power of the Holy Spirit within you has changed you as well. Satan has tried and will keep trying¾but dear child of God, trust in God's overwhelming love! (Isaiah 54:17) "No weapon forged against you will prevail, and you will refute every tongue that accuses you."

Adult eagles no longer need their parents. As children of God, we will no longer need the constant hand-holding that God may have done early on. Do not let this upset you, but rejoice! God is showing His confidence in your love and faithfulness to Him. Our hearts will tell on us. The Holy Spirit lives within us and will convict us when we do something that displeases Him. As you grow in Christ, the constant nudging He gives you should be fewer, but He speaks to you differently now more to direct you to help you in an area or to help someone else. You have more confidence in your relationship with Him, and it has grown even deeper. (I John 3:21-22) "Dear friends, if our hearts do not condemn us, we have confidence before God and receive from Him anything we ask, because we obey His commands and do what pleases Him." Talking to the Father has become automatic and brings your heart great joy. Rejoice in your growth and stand firm! A strong relationship with the Lord will keep your heart joyful. (Nehemiah 8:10)

"Do not grieve, for the joy of the Lord is your strength." As you grow in Christ, troubles and heartaches still come, but you know where to take them. They are to teach you further and direct you to higher grounds in Christ to grow the kingdom of God. (Acts 1:8) "But you will receive power when the Holy Spirit comes on you, and you will be my witnesses in Jerusalem, and in all Judea and Samaria and to the ends of the earth." If you die more and more to yourself and yield yourself completely to the Holy Spirit, more and more of His ever-changing power will shine through you.

If you have not received the baptism of the Holy Spirit, then ask. The baptism of the Holy Spirit is when Christ baptizes you with His spiritual fire¾not the indwelling, which happens the moment you receive Christ. (John 1:33-34) "The man on whom you see the Spirit come down and remain is He who will baptize with the Holy Spirit. I have seen and I testify that this is the Son of God." Man baptizes you with water, and Jesus baptizes you with the Spirit. (Luke 3:16) "He will baptize you with the Holy Spirit and with fire." This power is from above, for His purpose and to bring Him glory. We will discuss this more in the next chapter.

Both bald and golden eagles (and their feathers) are highly revered within the American Indian culture and religion. They have the deepest respect and represent honesty, truth, majesty, strength, courage, wisdom, power, and freedom. All this represents the traits of our Father, and with the Holy Spirit of Christ within us, it should be in us as well. As we mature, these traits will show more and more. Our goal should be to become more and more Christlike. In growing toward this, His love will grow as well attracting more and more people to us. When Jesus walked the earth, people were attracted to Him. As you let Christ shine through you, God will direct your steps in the path that He wants to lead you in. You just have to say "yes" and obey. He will help you to accomplish the rest. God will take you to higher ground helping you to soar ever higher, from glory to glory, so Christ will thoroughly shine through you to others.

13

An Eagle's Flight! An Adult Eagle At Last!

Finally an adult eagle! He is out on his own with his own nest, feeding himself and not depending on his parents any longer! So are you! You are still learning, for we will never stop learning, yet you have arrived! (Hebrews 5:13-14) "Anyone who lives on milk, being still an infant, is not acquainted with the teaching about righteousness. But solid food is for the mature, who by constant use have trained themselves to distinguish good from evil." You have witnessed all along, but now you are in the purpose God has called you to. Whether it is a pastor, singer, Sunday school teacher, missionary, evangelist, or on-the-job witness, you are walking to the destination God has called you to! Congratulations! Considering the trials and tests you have been through so far, that is an accomplishment. It has been the love and faithfulness of God and His mighty power that has kept you and brought you thus far, and your willingness to obey and surrender completely to Him. (Psalm 44:3) "It was not by their sword that they won the land, nor did their arm bring them victory; it was Your right hand, Your arm, and the light of Your face, for You loved them."

**The Great Seal of the
United States of
America**

The Great Seal of the United States of America is a symbol of sovereignty. It was adopted on June 20, 1782, by the Second Continental Congress. They chose the American Bald Eagle as the centerpiece of the Great Seal. It is due to the representation of the strength and the power of the Bald Eagle that it is chosen. The colors of the pales are those used in the flag of the United States of America. White, which signifies purity and innocence; red for hardiness and valor; and blue, the color of the Chief, signifies vigilance, perseverance, and justice. The olive branch and arrows denote the power of peace and war. In Christ, the red is His blood, for redemption in which He shed for us and is now the High Priest. (Hebrews 2:17-18) "For this reason, He had to be made like His brothers in every way, in order that He might become a merciful and faithful High Priest in service to God, and that He might make atonement for the sins of the people. Because He Himself suffered when He was tempted, He is able to help those who are being tempted." Blue, is the color of the Heavens in which He and the Father reside; white is for the purity that we all receive when we are washed clean by the blood of Christ. The eagle, its strength, and what it represents in this seal all portray the character of God. These same qualities are in every born-again Christian. They just need to grow. You are at the stage now that you are experiencing a harvest of the fruit of the Spirit. Keep standing firm and you will keep it growing.

The bald eagle is a symbol of strength and freedom¾being a child of God, we all possess these. Satan will try to rob you of that and make you doubt, but as long as you know that "every good and perfect gift is from above," he will never succeed. (Psalm 18:32-35) "It is God who arms me with strength and makes my way perfect. He makes my feet like the feet of a deer; He enables me to stand on the heights. He trains my hands for battle; my arms can bend a bow of bronze. You give me Your shield of victory, and Your right hand sustains me; You stoop down to make me great."

Eagles do not fly like other birds. Other birds flap their wings. This must be tiring. If we try to do everything on our own, we will be worn out physically and emotionally. That is what Satan tries to do to us. He tries to blindside us suddenly and catch us off guard so he can wear us out and ruin our walk and testimony in Christ. Even walking in the plan God has for you, you still need to be alert and feed on His Word daily. Eagles soar. They glide on the wind. That is what the Holy Spirit is for us. As we yield to Him, we will soar "on the wings of an eagle," "On the wings of our God." God will arm you with the strength to continue. (Philippians 4:13) "I can do everything through Him who gives me strength." As a mature Christian you have learned this, but as things start to go great for you, do not let your guard down. Stay close to God, not only in His Word but spending quality time with Him.

(Ephesians 5:15-17) "Be very careful, then, how you live—not as unwise but as wise, making the most of every opportunity, because the days are evil. Therefore do not be foolish, but understand what the Lord's will is." Now that you have arrived, Satan will try to busy your life so much you lose time with God. Don't let that happen. Keep your life God-centered and you will be just fine. (Ephesians 6:10-11) "Finally, be strong in the Lord and in His mighty power. Put on the full armor of God so that you can take your stand against the devil's schemes."

As you yield to the Holy Spirit, more of the Holy Spirit will flow through. That is the purpose of our walk¾to let Jesus shine through. He is the one who performs miracles. He will do it through you. Let the river flow, and it will abundantly. (John 7:38) "If anyone is thirsty, let him come to Me and drink. Whoever believes in Me, as the Scripture has said, streams of living water will flow from within him." Everyone that Jesus touched was healed.   He performed miracle after miracle. Where the river of the Holy Spirit flows, there is life! Everything comes to life! (Ezekiel 47:9) "There will be large numbers of fish because this water flows there and makes the salt water fresh; so where the river flows everything will live." If you have not been baptized in the Holy Spirit by now, ask! He gives freely. Some people receive the baptism immediately after they are saved, some do not. I believe it is a matter of yielding. For the power of the Holy Spirit to flow freely through you, you need to surrender totally to Him. That takes maturity in Christ, totally trusting Him, and His love for you. For some this is hard. For some, they are fearful of the baptism. On the night that Jesus was betrayed, a detachment of Roman soldiers was there, and all Jesus had to do was speak and they all fell over!

Now that is power! God is a jealous God and He will not give His glory to another. That may be the reason you have not received it yet. (Isaiah 42:8) "I am the Lord; that is My name! I will not give My glory to another or My praise to idols." Regardless, He gives His Spirit freely; He wants to, so ask! The power of the Holy Spirit will awaken new gifts in you, and it is all for the glory and the work of God the Father. (Psalm 89:13-18) "Your arm is endued with power; Your hand is strong, Your right hand is exalted. Righteousness and justice are the foundation of Your throne; love and faithfulness go before You. Blessed are those who have learned to acclaim You, who walk in the light of Your presence, O Lord. They rejoice in Your name all day long; they exult in Your righteousness. For You are their glory and strength, and by Your favor, You exalt our horn. Indeed, our shield belongs to the Lord, our king to the Holy One of Israel."

Elisha asked for a double portion of Elijah's anointing. (II Kings 2:9-11) "Let me inherit a double portion of your spirit,' Elisha replied. 'You have asked a difficult thing,' Elijah said, 'yet if you see me when I am taken from you, it will be yours otherwise not.' As they were walking along and talking together, suddenly a chariot of fire and horses of fire appeared and separated the two of them, and Elijah went up to heaven in a whirlwind."

We can receive a double portion as well. First at receiving the indwelling of His Spirit into our hearts at conversion, then at the baptism of the Holy Spirit in which we are totally filled with His Spirit and the power of the Spirit. We just need to see with our hearts, believe. This is what is symbolized when Elijah asks Elisha if he saw him when he was taken. The first baptisms were given to the disciples and then to the people they started preaching to. The disciples had to wait until Jesus ascended into heaven. (Acts 1:4-5) "Do not leave Jerusalem, but wait for the gift My Father promised, which you have heard Me speak about. For John baptized with water, but in a few days you will be baptized with the Holy Spirit." They waited on Him and received the baptism.

Keep asking and asking for God to show you areas that you have not surrendered to if you still haven't received it. It might just be a matter of waiting on Him and His timing. After all, He has probably waited a long time for you to receive Him and probably even longer to get to this point of maturity in your Christian walk. It is up to Jesus when we receive it. Some of the people the disciples preached to upon believing received it at once. (Acts 2:1-3) "When the day of Pentecost came, they were all together in one place. Suddenly a sound like the blowing of a violent wind came from heaven and filled the whole house where they were sitting. They saw what seemed to be tongues of fire that separated and came to rest on each of them." Each of us is different, and the Holy Spirit will come on us in the way He chooses. Keep praying and keep waiting. It is worth the wait! There may be different gifts birthed in you after the baptism that you are not already experiencing.

The gifts given to you upon being baptized by the Holy Spirit are for the good of all people, whether it is believers or unbelievers. No matter what gifts that we are blessed with, God works in all of them. (I Corinthians 12:6-11) "There are different kinds of working, but the same God works all of them in all men. Now to each one, the manifestation of the Spirit is given for the common good. To one there is given through the Spirit the message of wisdom, to another the message of knowledge by means of the same Spirit, to another faith by the same Spirit, to another other gifts of healing, by that one Spirit, to another miraculous powers, to another prophecy, to another distinguishing between spirits, to another speaking in different kinds of tongues, and to still another the interpretation of tongues. All these are the work of one and the same Spirit, and He gives them to each one just as He determines."

In this life, we will all have hardships. "He causes His sun to rise on the evil and the good, and sends rain on the righteous and the unrighteous." I don't know about you, but I would rather have God on my side than against me. (Matthew 12:30) "He who is not with Me is against Me, and he who does not gather with Me scatters." Continue your walk, striving daily to grow closer and closer, deeper and deeper in your relationship with God. He loves you so much and all you have to do is keep loving Him, and the love of Christ within your heart will compel you to do what is right. God does all the rest. (Psalm 103:2-5) "Praise the Lord, O my soul, and forget not all His benefits--who forgives all your sins and heals all your diseases, who redeems your life from the pit and crowns you with good things so that your youth is renewed like the eagle's."

Just surrender and trust, then ride on the wings of our God through life!

Epilogue

Our walk through life is not always easy. It will have ups and downs whether you are a Christian or not. The difference for Christians is we have a God who loves us so much He sent His One and Only Son to pay the price for our sins. The love of God within you will not only complete you, but it will give you confidence and help you to overcome anything. (I John 4:16-18) "And so we know and rely on the love God has for us. God is love. Whoever lives in love lives in God, and God in Him. In this way, love is made complete among us so that we will have confidence on the day of judgment because in this world we are like Him. There is no fear in love. But perfect love drives out fear because fear has to do with punishment. The one who fears is not made perfect in love." We have someone who gives us hope for the future and makes us feel loved when we are all alone in the world. God fills us so completely, that it gives us a contentment that will bear up under any situation. (Philippians 4:11-13) "For I have learned to be content whatever the circumstances. I know what it is to be in need, and I know what it is to have plenty. I have learned the secret of being content in any and every situation, whether well-fed or hungry, whether living in plenty or in want. I can do everything through Him who gives me strength."

It takes time to get to that point in your relationship with God. You have years of the world in you before you come to Him. Some things you will be delivered from the moment you receive Jesus and His forgiveness, but the rest will have to be worked out. You will be renewed day by day as you stay in the Word and walk through your tests and trials and not set up housekeeping! (II Corinthians 4:16) "Therefore we do not lose heart. Though outwardly we are wasting away, yet inwardly we are being renewed day by day." Just like teenagers growing up; they seem to think that they have it all figured out and their parents are all wrong and they just need to get a clue! Then after some ups and downs of their own and consequences to some very bad decisions, they finally realize that their parents are a little bit smarter than they gave them credit. So it is with the carnal mind that is a part of us all. Our minds need to be transformed. (Romans 12:2) "Do not conform any longer to the pattern of this world, but be transformed by the renewing of your mind." God does this through the tests and trials that we walk through. (James 1:2-4) "Consider it pure joy, my brothers, whenever you face trials of many kinds because you know that the testing of your faith develops perseverance. Perseverance must finish its work so that you may be mature and complete, not lacking anything."

He could snap His fingers and make everything perfect. But you wouldn't learn anything. We always learn from our mistakes if we have a sincere heart that wants to love and please God. (Psalm 25:4-5) "Show me Your ways, O Lord, teach me Your paths; guide me in Your truth and teach me, for you are God my Savior, and my hope is in You all day long." The Israelites proved this. God parted the Red Sea and destroyed the Egyptians who were following them as Moses led them out of Egypt. He made water come from a rock when they were traveling in the desert and parched with thirst, He rained down manna from heaven to feed them, His Spirit followed them in a cloud by day and fire by night, and He led them through one victory after another and they still would not have complete faith in Him. They kept doubting every time trouble came, and instead of remembering all the things He had done for them in the past, they chose the way of FEAR! Fear is not from God. (Romans 8:15-17) "For you did not receive a spirit of fear, but you received the Spirit of sonship. And by Him, we cry, 'Abba, Father.' The Spirit Himself testifies with our spirit that we are God's children. Now if we are children, then we are heirs¾heirs of God and co-heirs with Christ, if indeed we share in His sufferings in order that we may also share in His glory."

God gave us dominion and free will when He created us. A forced love is not a love that is worth having, nor will it be truly faithful. Would you want your husband, wife, girlfriend, boyfriend, or children to love you because you make them, or would you rather have a love of their own free will? God wants us to come to Him of our own free will as well. When we do, we will seek Him earnestly. God knows that when you seek Him with all your heart, you will want to obey Him, as you want your children to obey you, and you will want to read His Word. (Hebrews 11:6) "And without faith it is impossible to please God because anyone who comes to Him must believe that He exists and that He rewards those who earnestly seek Him."

When you courted your spouse, you dated first to get to know each other and grew to love each other unconditionally. That is the kind of love that God has for us, and He wants it back in return. (John 4:24) "God is spirit, and His worshipers must worship Him in spirit and in truth." God's Word is powerful. If He could use it to create the world, and if Jesus could use it when He was going through His time of testing in the desert, then it is certainly good enough for us. We need to stop being lazy Christians expecting God to hand everything to us on a silver platter and grow up spiritually! You expect nothing less from your own children! Should God be any different with us? No! If you truly love your children, you let them learn from their mistakes. They will not want to keep making them if you discipline them and let them learn from them. Disciplining is a part of loving your children. It helps them to grow and to learn right from wrong. God as our heavenly Father will do the same for us because He loves us. (Hebrews 12:5-7) "My son, do not make light of the Lord's discipline and do not lose heart when He rebukes you, because the Lord disciplines those He loves, and He punishes everyone He accepts as a son. Endure hardship as discipline; God is treating you as sons." You should never doubt God's love. The sacrifice of Jesus should be all the proof you need. (John 15:12-13) "My command is this: Love each other as I have loved you. Greater love has no one than this, that he lay down his life for his friends." Most people on Earth will only love you if you love them back. Not with God. He loves us deep in sin and washed in the blood of Jesus. (Romans 5:8) "But God demonstrates His own love for us in this: While we were still sinners, Christ died for us."

As you receive Jesus and take flight in the arms of our God, remember to trust Him always. This will give you great peace. (Philippians 4: 6-7) "Do not be anxious about anything, but in everything, by prayer and petition, with thanksgiving, present your requests to God. And the peace of God, which transcends all understanding, will guard your hearts and your minds in Christ Jesus."

Have you ever had the privilege of having someone pay a bill for you or tell you "no charge?" Well, that is what God did for us. He looked at all the sins in the world and knew that it was just too much. We could not pay for it. (Isaiah 59:16-17) "He saw that there was no one, He was appalled that there was no one to intervene; so His own arm worked salvation for Him, and His own righteousness sustained Him. He put on the righteousness as His breastplate, and the helmet of salvation on His head; He put on the garments of vengeance and wrapped Himself in zeal as in a cloak." After He looked at all the sin and compared it to the overwhelming love that He has for us, through Jesus He says, "NO CHARGE!" It should give you overwhelming peace. Would anyone else in the entire world love you so completely that for anything that you could ever do they would forgive you and tell you "no charge?" Psalm 91 below tells the story of God's love. His love is comfort, refuge, renewal, protection, deliverance, and salvation.

"He who dwells in the shelter of the Most High will rest in the shadow of the Almighty. I will say of the Lord, 'He is my refuge and my fortress, my God, in whom I trust.' Surely He will save you from the fowler's snare and from the deadly pestilence. He will cover you with His feathers, and under His wings you will find refuge; His faithfulness will be your shield and rampart. You will not fear the terror of night, nor the arrow that flies by day, nor the pestilence that stalks in the darkness, nor the plague that destroys at midday. A thousand may fall at your side, ten thousand at your right hand, but it will not come near you. You will only observe with your eyes and see the punishment of the wicked. If you make the Most High your dwelling--even the Lord, who is my refuge- then no harm will befall you, no disaster will come near your tent. For He will command His angels concerning you to guard you in all your ways; they will lift you up in their hands, so that you will not strike your foot against a stone. You will tread upon the lion and the cobra; you will trample the great lion and the serpent. 'Because he loves Me,' says the Lord, I will rescue him; I will protect him, for he acknowledges My name. He will call upon Me, and I will answer him; I will be with him in trouble, I will deliver him and honor him. With long life will I satisfy him and show him My salvation."

Take me away from this world and into Your presence, it is where I feel at home, it is where I belong.
It is where I've belonged all along.

Hide me in the shadow of Your wings guide me in the light of Your path,
it is there that Your joy and peace reside in me and keep me forever free!

Take me away Lord and hide me in Your wings. Shine Your love into my heart and Your praises I will sing.

Take me away O Lord I pray. Hide me in the shadow of Your presence every day!

Special Invitation

I cannot close this book without giving you the awesome privilege of becoming a child of God, a chance to have every wrong made right and every sin washed away. If you have never asked Jesus into your heart, or maybe you did but you were never sincere, please pray the prayer on the pages following. It will be the best thing you have ever done.

After you do this, find a good Church to go to if you do not have one already. Fellowshipping with other Christians will help you on your new walk in Christ. It is also a place to worship God and learn more about Him. Also, tell someone! You must confess! This should be the happiest day of your life because you now know that your eternal home is in heaven! That is the best life insurance anyone can have, and it is free!

(Romans 10:9-10) "That if you confess with your mouth, 'Jesus is Lord,' and believe in your heart that God raised Him from the dead, you will be saved. For it is with your heart that you believe and are justified, and it is with your mouth that you confess and are saved."

Congratulations and welcome to the family of God!

God Loves You!

(Jeremiah. 31:3) "I have loved you with an everlasting love; I have drawn you with loving-kindness."

I Timothy 2:3-4 "God our Savior, who wants all men to be saved and to come to the knowledge of the truth."

He will not knock on the door of your heart forever. Will you let Him in?

Revelation 3:20 "Here I am! I stand at the door and knock. If anyone hears My voice and opens the door, I will come in and eat with him, and he with Me."

Jesus is the only way to God.
John 14:6 "I am the way, the truth, and the life. No one comes to the Father except through Me."

John 3:3 "I tell you the truth, no one can see the kingdom of God unless he is born again."

And you must make Him Lord of your life.
Matthew 6:24 "No one can serve two masters."
Matthew 7:21 "Not everyone who says to Me, 'Lord, Lord', will enter the kingdom of heaven, but only he who does the will of My Father who is in heaven."

We must leave our old ways behind.
Mark 3:25 "If a house is divided against itself, that house cannot stand."

You can't live according to the flesh and desires of the sinful nature and expect to have Jesus in your heart. He is holy. He is love. Love and Hate cannot exist together.

Ephesians 4:22-24 "You were taught, with regard to your former way of life, to put off your old self, which is being corrupted by its deceitful desires; to be made new in the attitude of your minds; and to put on the new self, created to be like God in true righteousness and holiness."

God gives you the ability to do His will. He knows it is hard.
Philippians 4:13 "I can do everything through Him who gives me strength."

Romans 3:23 "For all have sinned and fall short of the glory of God."

I John 1:9 "If we confess our sins, He is faithful and just and will forgive us our sins and purify us from all unrighteousness."

John 1:12 "Yet to all who received Him, to those who believed in His name, He gave the right to become children of God."

Romans 10:10 "For it is with your heart that you believe and are justified, and it is with your mouth that you confess and are saved."

Then after you confess and ask forgiveness and receive Jesus into your heart, you must testify (tell someone) and be baptized. In this, God is glorified, and others might be saved by your example.

II Timothy 1:8 "So do not be ashamed to testify about our Lord"

I Peter 3:21 "And this water symbolizes baptism that now saves you also- not the removal of dirt from the body but the pledge of a good conscience toward God. It saves you by the resurrection of Jesus Christ."

Invitation To Salvation Prayer

Dear Almighty Father in heaven, I know that I am a sinner and I ask your forgiveness of all my sins. I want to make You the Lord of my life and I want to serve You all the days of my life. I believe that Jesus Christ died on the cross for my sins.

Thank you so much for loving me and waiting for me to come to the knowledge of the truth! Thank you for my salvation. Please help me and guide me in learning your Word so I can be a light to the world. Please, Jesus, come into my heart and baptize me with your Holy Spirit. I thank You and praise Your Holy Name and ask all this in the name of Jesus Christ our Lord. Amen.

Other Books By Sandra (Lott) Smith

Adult Books

Jeremy's Journey
Safe In Papa's Hands
Her Final Curtain
Deep Waters Within
Deep Waters Rage: Sequel to Deep Waters Within
My Father's Eyes: Seeing Yourself Through The Eyes of Love
Hannah: From Barren to Blossom
Ride the Wind
A Princess in Waiting
The Princess in the Harlot
Step By Step Into A Deeper Walk In Christ
I'm Saved! Where Do I Go From Here?
The Day Hope Was Born: God's Gift of Love
The Holy Spirit and the Baptism of the Holy Spirit
Repairing Broken Walls: Restoring Joy & Peace-The Book
Repairing Broken Walls: Restoring Joy & Peace-The Study Guide
Jewels From the Word & Manna For the Soul
Captivated By God's Love: Poems From the Heart
You've Got This: Learning To Let Go
I'm Saved! What Next? Beginning Your Walk In Christ
The Father He Never Knew He Needed
In the Garden with Jesus
Princess Anastasia & the Kingdom of Divulgence

Children's Books

The Sheep That Went Astray
Naomi's Joy
Molly's Journey to Forgiveness
Tim & Gerald Ray Series: The Wind Has a Voice
Tim & Gerald Ray Series: How Did He Get in There?
Tim & Gerald Ray Series: A Light in the Sky
Tim & Gerald Ray Series: Let's Go Swimming
Tim & Gerald Ray Series: Blowing in the Wind
Tim & Gerald Ray Series: Summer on Grandma's Farm
Sassy Goes Exploring

Sandra (Lott) Smith was born and raised in San Antonio, Texas, with one sister and two brothers. Sandra loves the mountains, making candles, and jewelry. She is the author of Jeremy's Journey, Deep Waters Within, A Princess in Waiting, Ride the Wind, and more. She has also written children's such as, The Wind Has a Voice and How Did He Get in There, Molly's Journey to Forgiveness, and more. She has written over 38 books to date and began writing poetry as soon as she was saved in June 1998. The Lord gave her, her first book to write right after her son was killed. Writing was not something she sought out. She poured her heart into time spent with the Lord in order to allow Him to heal her heart and the name of her first book was birthed in her spirit along with the chapters and what it was to be about during a devotion time. It was called: God's Love; ironically enough, with all that she was going through, God's love was exactly what she needed.

She is passionate about studying the Bible. She has taught Sunday school, and Bible Study Groups, assists in preaching in her present church, and served in the Celebrate Recovery Ministry, and Homeless Outreach. Sandra was also interviewed on radio shows such as Golden Life Living and WMAP Radio (World's Most Amazing People based out of New York), the Bill Martinez show, and a Fox Radio show called the Kim Kennedy Show.

She is a devoted mother of 2 sons (Tim & Gerald Ray), Gerald Ray the youngest, has gone on to be with the Lord due to a car accident. Through the death of her youngest son at the age of 16, a rocky marriage to an alcoholic and the abuse that came with that, and other overwhelming trials, she has drawn close to the loving arms of the Father. Experiencing God's unconditional love as He held her heart in His hands, has created a passion in her to help others grow in their understanding of and receive God's love and grow spiritually. She has the heart to help hurting women discover the princess in Christ that they truly are and overcome abuse. She teaches on topics to help you reach spiritual maturity, persevere through the hard times, and how to reach your destiny in Christ!